About the Author

As a parent of a non-verbal, young man with autism, Deanna Picon personally understands the impact of autism on a family. She knows first-hand how heartbreaking a diagnosis of autism can be for parents and the personal struggles that often follow.

But, through her own journey with autism, Deanna also recognizes the special joys, rewarding experiences and unique life gifts which can result from raising a child with special needs.

Deanna established **YOUR AUTISM COACH, LLC** to help parents successfully meet the distinctive challenges of raising autistic and special needs children. Her company provides a comprehensive program of personalized guidance and support for parents, along with seminars that give parents coping strategies and proven techniques to maintain a healthy, emotional outlook.

Her personal mission is to empower parents as they advocate for their children, while balancing productive work and family lives.

Deanna brings over 20 years of professional coaching and management development experience to her work, including roles at major Fortune 500 companies such as McGraw-Hill, American Express and Avon Products. She has coached, trained and advised business professionals from senior corporate executives to individual entrepreneurs and small business owners.

Her academic credentials include a Bachelor of Arts degree in Psychology and a Bachelor of Arts degree in Broadcast Journalism from Syracuse University. She is a graduate of the Management Training and Development Diploma Program from New York University's Management Training Institute.

Deanna lives in New York City with her husband and son. She can be reached through her website at www.YourAutismCoach.com.

Cover design: Unauthorized Media
Cover photographs courtesy of Shutterstock

Library of Congress Cataloging-In-Publication Data has been applied for.

ISBN – 13: 978-1497581227

ISBN – 10: 1497581222

Printed in the United States of America

This book is dedicated to parents everywhere, particularly the parents of children with autism, who step up to the plate every day and do their best for their children. None of us is perfect, but all of you are awesome!

I would not have written this book, or even been here in one piece today, if it were not for some very special people:

My incredible parents, Kenneth and Lucille, who gave me strength when I needed it most and whose love and encouragement I will be eternally grateful for;

My wonderful husband, Tony, who has been a supportive partner, great father and a bottomless well of compassion and dedication;

And my amazing son, Lorenzo, who has taught me that true love needs no words, and that there is nothing parents won't do to give their children a good and rewarding life. Mommy and Daddy are so proud of you.

Special, heartfelt thanks to my dear friends, Toni and Glen, for their unwavering belief in me and help with this book. You're the best!

Contents

INTRODUCTION   1

   FOR ONCE, IT'S ALL ABOUT <u>YOU</u>   2

1 - WHAT'S HAPPENED TO YOU   5

   DIAGNOSIS – The Day Your Life Changed Forever   6

   THE FORGOTTEN PARENTS – Left Behind In the Autism Wilderness   7

   THE ROLLER COASTER EFFECT – Understanding Your Emotions   8

   THE FIVE STAGES – Dealing With Your Reactions   10

   NUCLEAR SIDE EFFECTS – Believe It or Not, This is Normal!   13

   YOUR TRIGGERS – What Sets Off Nuclear Side Effects   16

   YOUR OWN DIAGNOSIS – Autism Parents' Spectrum Disorder   17

2 - HOW TO ADAPT TO YOUR NEW LIFE   21

   WHAT NOW? – Addressing Your New Reality   22

   FAMILY IMPACTS – How Autism Affects Everyone   24

   HELPING YOURSELVES – Family Summits   28

   LIFE TOGETHER – You and Your Child   30

   MANAGING EXPECTATIONS – Be Positive but Realistic   32

   YOU ARE AN A+ PARENT – Take Pride in Your Family   39

   THE FIX-IT TOUR – Answers, Not Cures   39

3 - BUILDING YOUR AUTISM BATTLE PLAN   44

   BATTLE PLAN? – Yes, Because This is War!   45

   START WITH YOURSELF – Shift Your Mindset and <u>KNOW</u> You Can Win   49

   YOU AND YOUR PARTNER – Co-Supporters & Team Leaders   56

   YOU AND YOUR AUTISTIC CHILD – The Battle of the Bond   62

   YOU AND YOUR OTHER CHILDREN – Autism's Sneak Attack   67

   YOU AND YOUR FAMILY AND FRIENDS – Don't Let the Bonds Break   71

   YOU AND YOUR CHILD'S EDUCATION – Don't Be Overwhelmed   74

   YOU AND YOUR ADVISORY COUNCIL – Tapping Your Power Resources   81

   YOU AND YOUR BATTLE PLAN – Be the General!   84

CONCLUSION - DID I TELL YOU HOW AMAZING YOU ARE?   86

   TAKE A BOW – You Deserve It!   87

INTRODUCTION

FOR ONCE, IT'S ALL ABOUT <u>YOU</u>

The last time I looked, Amazon.com offered more than 12,000 books about autism; everything from advice and theories to memoirs and cookbooks.

So, why do we need another autism book?

The answer is simple – this book is <u>not</u> about autism. It is about <u>you</u>, the parent of a child with autism.

Why I Wrote This Book

I'm one of you.

My son, who is now 18, has autism and is non-verbal. He is also sweet, wonderful and the complete owner of my heart. And even though I've never heard him speak one word, when I look into his eyes, I know he feels the same way about me.

Like so many parents in our situation, I found it extremely difficult having a child with autism. When he was first diagnosed, I didn't think I'd make it 18 days, much less 18 years.

But here I am – still standing, still advocating for my son and, more importantly, not alone.

And along the way, I learned something very important. When it comes to a family touched by autism, parents need guidance and support too.

Tony, Deanna & Lorenzo Picon

So, I've made it my mission to use my professional experience as an autism coach to **empower** parents.

We have to be proactive about seeking treatment for our children, but also realistic enough to know when we need help ourselves.

You Have Special Needs, Too

More than doctors, therapists, educators and other experts, parents are the key to the quality of life for any child. That goes double for a child with autism.

You are their link to the world, their protectors, their advocates, their caregivers and the source of love and affection that all children need and deserve.

INTRODUCTION

So, who is taking care of <u>you</u>?

What about <u>your</u> special needs, as parents taking on a life-long challenge, facing unknown trials ahead?

Who can understand what you're going through and help you get through it?

This isn't about feeling sorry for yourself or failing to put your child first. It's about realizing that parenting a child with autism can be very tough, and you will need to be at the top of your game.

If you can recognize and deal with your own challenges as parents, you'll be better able to give your child the best life possible.

Not to mention, preserve your sanity!

What's In This Book

It's taken me 18 years of personal experience, professional training and working with hundreds of parents to teach me what I know today.

This book takes all of those lessons and puts them into strategies that you can use.

It also contains the real-life advice that I desperately wish someone had given <u>me</u> 18 years ago!

And although this book represents the life lessons I've learned during my continuing journey with autism, I know all parents' experiences will be unique, just like their children and their personal situations.

The commonality of our experiences is the thread that binds us all together.

Section One – What's Happened to You

This section will help you understand how the diagnosis of your child has affected you and the impact it may have on your life.

The main point, which I really could have used all those years ago, is that an autism diagnosis is devastating. And it's completely normal for you to feel like you've lost control of your life as you come to grips with what autism means for you and your child.

You're experiencing what I call the "Autism Parents' Spectrum Disorder" – the emotional, mental and social shockwaves created by that bombshell diagnosis of autism. And the sooner you realize this, the closer you can come to reclaiming your life.

There is a feeling of disbelief that comes over you, that takes over, and you kind of go through the motions. You do what you're supposed to do, but in fact you're not there at all. – Writer & editor Frederick Barthelme

Section Two – How to Adapt to Your New Life

Reading this section will assist you in recognizing how the diagnosis has affected your partner, your immediate family, your friends and your future. You'll realize that you are <u>not</u> alone, <u>not</u> facing an impossible challenge and <u>not</u> destined to a life of doom and gloom.

Most importantly, this section will help you avoid the most common pitfalls and mental traps that plague parents in our situation.

Instead of wasting time and energy on the pointless and negative, you will be able to focus on the productive and positive.

Section Three – Building Your Autism Battle Plan

Once you have the tools of knowledge and understanding in your hands, Section Three will provide a blueprint for your own Autism Battle Plan.

This part of the book will focus on how you can prevent autism from defining or defeating you ... how to keep hold of your self-identity and your relationships ... and how to not only survive but actually <u>enjoy</u> raising your special child.

> *No matter how calmly you try to referee, parenting will eventually produce bizarre behavior, and I'm <u>not</u> talking about the kids ...*
> - Comedian Bill Cosby

In other words, <u>how to reclaim your life</u>.

This Book Is For You

Whether you've just been handed the diagnosis, or you've been dealing with the autism challenge for years, you will find help in these pages.

Whether you are determined, scared, or simply feeling a bit numb and overwhelmed, you will see that there is hope.

And whether you are a family member, friend or professional, you will learn how to understand and support the parents of special needs children.

Nobody ever gets the life they expected. But, with a little assistance and a positive outlook, we can make the best of the life we have been given.

You and your family can have a <u>good</u> life – as good as any other family.

I want to show you how, so let's get started!

Deanna Picon
Founder, *Your Autism Coach, LLC*

PART 1

WHAT'S HAPPENED TO YOU

DIAGNOSIS – The Day Your Life Changed Forever

YOUR CHILD HAS AUTISM

Those are the words no parent ever wants to hear. Who would have thought that four little words could turn your world upside down and inside out?

For most parents, the devastating blow comes after weeks, months or even years of wondering if there is "something wrong" with your child, and being terrified of the answer.

It may follow a long period of searching, hoping, denying, wishing and fearing, or it may strike you like lightning out of a clear blue sky.

But, sooner or later, a pediatrician, pediatric neurologist or another autism specialist drops the bomb on you and your family.

It's like your own personal 9/11 – you'll never forget where you were, how you heard the news or the way it made you feel.

> *This isn't just life in the fast lane, this is life in the oncoming traffic.*
> *— Author Terry Pratchett*

Your reality has just disappeared and been replaced with another – one that you don't recognize and, certainly, didn't expect. Those four little words have changed your life forever.

YOU'VE JUST BEEN HIT BY A TRUCK!

It's a lovely, sunny day and you and your child are driving along a quiet country road. Your child is safely strapped in, you're both wearing your seatbelts and there's no sign of danger.

Out of nowhere, a truck side swipes your car, skidding it off the road and into a telephone pole. Everyone is stunned by the impact.

You watch, dazed, as emergency workers arrive at the scene and slowly help you and your child out of the car. You stand and respond to their questions about the accident, although you have no idea what you're saying. All you remember is getting in the ambulance and riding to the hospital.

At the hospital, you are directed to the waiting room. With your nerves on a razor's edge, you wait while your child undergoes tests and assessments.

You sit down in the chair and suddenly, it dawns on you … why aren't they treating me? Why hasn't anyone taken me into the emergency room for observation?

I was hit by that truck as well, and I have been hurt by the collision, but where is my treatment?

And you silently think to yourself … don't they know how much pain I'm in? I have internal injuries. My heart is bleeding and my spirit is broken. I have shattered hopes and dreams.

Where is everyone? I need some help, too!

Okay – so, now what?

You've just heard something that's hard to believe and process.

You may feel numb, or go into denial, or rant and rage, or behave in some other way that you might regret or feel ashamed of afterwards.

> *When you forgive, you in no way change the past, but you sure do change the future.*
> – Radio host Bernard Meltzer

That's a normal reaction to shock on this scale. Forgive yourself if you didn't react the way you would have liked to, and extend that forgiveness to your partner, family members and close friends.

Very few people react well when they've just been hit by a truck!

You, and others around you, will need time, support and patience to get over this initial shock.

The parents of a child diagnosed with autism face a special challenge, because they often get lost in the aftermath of the bombshell ...

THE FORGOTTEN PARENTS – Left Behind In the Autism Wilderness

When a diagnosis of autism is confirmed, it's like a hurricane centered on your child. There is a huge amount of activity and everything else is swept away – only the focus on the child remains.

Obviously, a young girl or boy with special needs deserves to have special attention. But this immediate focus often becomes permanent; nobody thinks of anyone or anything else, now or in the long term.

Most of the time, the parents are offered plenty of support and resources for their child, but none for themselves. Instead, they are expected to immediately process and accept what is happening, and to "stay strong" for their son or daughter.

> *The world breaks everyone. But, afterwards, some are stronger in the broken places.*
> – Author Ernest Hemingway

Few people ever seem to realize that parents in this situation have special needs, too.

This often sets the pattern for the parents, putting the child as the number one priority and themselves as a very distant second.

That's not a way of life that can be maintained. It's a trap, and a recipe for burn-out. Yet many parents never break free of that pattern.

WELCOME TO THE DEEP END

When the doctor finally comes out into the waiting room, she explains what is wrong and what needs to be done.

"Here's the diagnosis of your child, here's the prescription, here's the list of treatment options, here are the specialists you should consult ..." the doctor goes on loading your hands with papers and your overwrought brain with information.

As she begins to walk away, the doctor suddenly stops and says, "Oh, yes, I almost forgot – this is for you!"

Gratefully, you take the prescription slip she's offering you. At last, someone is providing you with some support and guidance!

But, when you read the slip of paper, it simply says "Welcome to the World of Autism".

You have a lapful of information, support and suggestions for your child, but nothing to help guide yourself.

Like most parents of newly-diagnosed children, you feel forgotten and lost in the autism wilderness without a map or compass.

THE ROLLER COASTER EFFECT – Understanding Your Emotions

So, how <u>should</u> things have gone for you that day? What could have made a difference and helped you better handle that hammer blow?

How about a scenario like this:

NOW, ABOUT YOU ...

After the doctor comes to you in the waiting room and explains how they will treat your child's condition, she invites you into her office.

"I know this is a horrible time for you," she says, "and I can see you are suffering from shock and emotional injury. So, while we all do what's right for your child, let's talk about the treatment for YOU."

The doctor reassures you that having strong emotional and even physical reactions to an autism diagnosis is perfectly normal, and that you should expect to go up and down, from weak to strong, in the weeks ahead.

"Everyone reacts a bit differently," she explains, "but here are the stages you will likely go through as you ride that emotional roller coaster..."

Those ten minutes could have made all the difference for you and others in our situation.

Well, since you didn't get that talk on the fateful day of diagnosis, here it is now ...

The Stages of Grief

A lot of people will tell you that you are going through "changes" following the diagnosis, but that's not true. What you're going through are "stages" – the classic stages of grief.

You may have heard of this idea, first described by psychiatrist Elizabeth Kübler-Ross. In her ground-breaking work, Dr. Kübler-Ross said people facing a terminal illness go through five stages of grief:

- **Denial – Refusing to believe what is happening**

- **Anger – Feeling that life is unfair and/or that someone or something can be blamed**

- **Bargaining – Wanting to make a deal or sacrifice that will somehow save you**

- **Depression – A loss of hope, energy, purpose, joy and ability to cope**

- **Acceptance – Facing up to reality and becoming determined to deal with it**

You may wonder why <u>you</u> would be going through these stages. Nobody's dying, after all.

While a diagnosis of autism is not a death sentence, it does represent an enormous loss for the parents.

- **The loss of the "perfect child" they dreamed about and hoped for**

- **The loss of the life they expected to live with their family**

- **The loss of the fun, freedom and flexibility they had in their lives before the child was born**

As with any other major loss, it's natural for people to go through the stages of grief in different orders, at different speeds, and even to repeat a stage or get stuck in one for a long time.

It's a long and difficult roller coaster ride for your thoughts and emotions.

Autism's Extra Burdens

The parents of a child with autism may have to cope with other, unique emotional losses –

- **Some parents may feel that their child is "lost" or even "dead", even though he/she is still physically present**

- **Parents whose child started out developing normally and then regressed face the grief of knowing what might have been, but has now been lost**

If a child dies, parents receive an outpouring of support and comfort. Those parents are <u>expected</u> to grieve and people will understand and make allowances for them.

> *Tears shed for another person are not a sign of weakness. They are a sign of a pure heart.* – Author José N. Harris

Sadly, few people will understand that you, too, are in the stages of grieving. Instead of empathy, you're more likely to have people expect you to "struggle" with the situation for a while and then move on with your life.

THE FIVE STAGES – Dealing With Your Reactions

Even if other people don't "get it", you **now** know what's going on in your heart and head – you're grieving, and you have every right to do so.

Knowing that you are going through the grief process allows you to better understand the strong feelings and negative thoughts you may be having now, or may have had in the past.

Some parents, particularly of older children or adults with autism, have experienced these stages for years and never knew it. Maybe you've already been through all or most of them.

Whatever your situation, this knowledge will help allow you to forgive yourself for those thoughts and feelings, just as you would make allowances for other people who are grieving.

So, let's take a closer look at those five stages and the kinds of reactions they can spark in the parents of recently-diagnosed children …

DENIAL

Obviously, there has been a mistake because my child is perfectly fit and healthy. These doctors aren't always right, and they have misdiagnosed my child. It can't possibly be autism – maybe there's a learning problem or something, but it is definitely <u>not</u> autism.

Sound familiar? Usually the first stage of grief that parents go through is complete or partial denial of the situation.

> *We protect ourselves by refusing to know ourselves.* – Artist Floriano Martins

Denial provides a "protective shield" for you. It's a natural defense mechanism that helps you handle feelings that are hard to deal with.

Unfortunately, a lot of people become stuck in this stage, sometimes for years.

After you get through this stage, you may look back and feel you were blind to what was happening right in front of you. But don't beat yourself up about it. You couldn't see what was happening because you couldn't handle it. Your denial protected you.

Now, it's time to move on. Only after you get past this stage can you start helping your child, your family and yourself.

ANGER

Anger can present itself in a lot of ways. You may be outraged that this happened to you and your child, while others may play the "blame game" – that's when you decide that someone is responsible for your child's autism.

You could be blaming yourself, your spouse, a family member, doctors, teachers or anyone else under the sun.

> *It is wise to direct your anger towards problems – not people; to focus your energies on answers – not excuses.*
> *– Evangelist William Arthur Ward*

The bottom line is the same in any case – you're wasting your time and energy because <u>no one</u> is to blame. Nobody <u>caused</u> your child to have autism.

> *There are two things a person should never be angry at, what they can help, and what they cannot*
> *– Ancient Greek philosopher Plato*

By holding on to your anger and directing it where it doesn't belong, you only end up hurting yourself by damaging your relationships and friendships.

There's another kind of anger you may be feeling – anger at the <u>situation</u> you're now in.

Let's face it; you may have to make some serious adjustments in your life to accommodate your child's disability -

- **You may have to quit work, change jobs or work only part-time in order to have enough hours at home with your child**

- **You may have to get a second job or take on more difficult work in order to help pay for the additional services your child needs**

- **Your finances may suffer because of lost income and increased expenses for adaptive equipment, home care and therapy**

- **You may have to change home and living arrangements or reduce time spent on hobbies or with friends, or cut back on vacations and social activities and a thousand other aspects of life**

Is it any wonder that you might feel angry? It's an understandable reaction to a very tough situation that demands a good deal of change.

It may help to know that you're right … it <u>isn't</u> fair that this happened to your child. It isn't fair for <u>any</u> family. But all the anger in the world won't change the situation, and you've got more important, productive uses for your time and energy.

BARGAINING

A good parent would do whatever is necessary for their child – throw him or herself on railroad tracks, stop a bullet with their body, or … if they somehow could … take a disability away from their child at any price.

That's why it is common for parents to go through a bargaining stage on their journey through grief. You are offering to do anything to help your child, no matter what the cost.

Often, people in our situation try to play "Let's Make A Deal" with God or Fate or the universe in general. You may promise to go to church every Sunday, be a better person, give all of your money to charity or even lay down your very life.

> *Bargaining with God is pointless. He already has a thousand followers that will do what you bargained to do for free.*
> – Author & counselor Shannon L. Alder

Anything, as long as the higher power you're bargaining with will make your child okay again.

As I said, a good parent would do whatever is necessary for their child. So, trying to make these bargains is simply evidence that you are a good parent in a bad situation.

Understand that you're not alone in the desperation you're feeling. We've all been there – sometimes more than we'd like to admit.

DEPRESSION

It's okay to feel sad about your situation; it would be strange if you didn't feel sadness about it now and then.

Just keep an eye out for sadness becoming deep depression. A deeply depressed person loses their energy, their 'spark', their hope, their interest in other people or life in general. Everything feels like a struggle and every day seems pointless.

This is another one of those stages that parents may be trapped in for a long time. What may start out as a normal emotional state can lead to a serious, downward spiral. When that happens, there's no point in trying to "snap out of it" – you need help.

A short book like this is no place to talk about all of the signs, effects and treatments for depression.

> *No matter what happens, or how bad it seems today, life does go on, and it will be better tomorrow.*
> – Writer Maya Angelou

The most important point is this: if you find yourself feeling more than sadness or lost in a deep depression, don't let it get worse. Talk to a doctor, therapist, counselor or mental health professional right away.

ACCEPTANCE

This is the stage where we come to terms with the diagnosis, adjust to reality and focus on having the best life possible for our families.

For the first time, you actually feel like you have some control over the situation. But the best part is, when you look at your child, you see a <u>person</u> and not a <u>disability</u>!

Getting to the point of Acceptance means having positive thoughts about your present situation and, even, hopeful feelings about the future. You may think --

- **"It's alright now. I can deal with my child's autism and the challenges ahead."**
- **"This isn't the life I planned as a parent, but I'm okay with it now."**
- **"This isn't the child I dreamed of, but I love him/her with all my heart."**

If you're still in one of the other four stages of grief, Acceptance may seem a long way away. But you can get there with time, patience, support and determination.

You may find yourself going through some stages more than once, in a completely different order, or feeling some stages more strongly than others. We're all different and need to grieve in our own ways.

> *The harder you fall, the heavier your heart; the heavier your heart, the stronger you climb; the stronger you climb, the higher your pedestal.*
> – Singer, poet and philosopher Criss Jami

And, while we all go through grief, we can <u>choose</u> to come out of it as stronger, kinder, better people, filled with compassion and a sense of purpose.

NUCLEAR SIDE EFFECTS – Believe It or Not, This is Normal!

Whether or not you go through all of the five stages of grief covered in the last section, you're bound to suffer from some of the side effects of dealing with the arrival of autism in your world.

Each of these may hit you like a ten megaton bomb, which is why I call them "<u>nuclear</u> side effects".

Between the initial shock of diagnosis, the stages of grief and these nuclear side effects, parents often feel like they are losing control or failing to cope with their new reality.

Well, guess what? These are all common, normal feelings. Your mind is facing quite a challenge – trying to adjust to a difficult situation.

> *If you want to make God laugh, tell him about your plans.* – Comedian & film director Woody Allen

That's not easy and these nuclear side effects can sneak up on you without warning and interfere with your clear thinking.

It will help if you recognize where your particular challenges lie and which nuclear side effects are most common for you. Knowing what is going on, and why it's happening, is half the battle. It's easier to deal with known problems instead of with a vague feeling that something is wrong.

So, as you look inside yourself to see how you're handling the stages of grief, keep an eye out for what else may be affecting you at the same time …

ISOLATION

Feeling like you are disconnected from the world or want to retreat into a shell?

Isolation can hit you on the emotional level, so that you "tune out" the other people around you and refuse to connect with them. It can also be physical, with parents staying at home, literally hiding out and not socializing with other people.

If you look at families playing in the park or interacting on TV and feel like you live on a different, painful and lonely planet, you're probably dealing with isolation.

DESPERATION

A couple of pages back we covered the idea of "bargaining" – trying to make a deal with a higher power to rescue your child from autism.

> *When things go bad, don't go with them.* – Singer & actor Elvis Presley

That's one way of expressing desperation. Another is to decide that you're going to be the one who finds the answer, the cure, the miracle that will somehow erase the diagnosis and "fix" your child.

It's one thing to do your research and get the latest information, but convincing yourself that there is one magic therapy, diet or other intervention to reverse autism is desperation at work.

GUILT

Mothers of children with autism will often put themselves through the wringer, wondering if they did something to "cause" their child's disability. Was it something they did during the pregnancy? Something they failed to do? Some kind of judgment or punishment?

Fathers may look at their genetic history and the role they played in the birth and early months of their child. Do they have "bad" genes? Did they fail to pick up on some clue? Could they have done something better or different that would have prevented this?

Guilt can eat away at your self-image, undermine your relationships and leave you feeling hopeless and helpless. It's hard not to feel guilty, even when you know it is not logical or helpful. It may be a phase that you have to get through on the road to Acceptance.

> *There's no problem so bad that you can't add some guilt to it and make it even worse.* – Cartoonist Bill Watterson

CONFUSION

There's nothing like being bombarded with tons of medical information, complicated scientific lingo and contradictory advice from everyone you know ... right at the most stressful time of your life!

Many parents will feel confused or overwhelmed – not only following the diagnosis, but off and on at many times in their lives.

> *Each person has two wolves fighting inside them. One is evil, full of jealousy, hate, regret and anger. The other is good, full of forgiveness, peace, kindness and faith. Which one wins the fight? It depends on which one you feed.*
> *– Traditional Cherokee folk story*

Don't be surprised or alarmed if it happens to you or someone close to you. Sometimes, we need to take a breath, step back and deal with one thing at a time.

HOPELESSNESS

Few things are harder for a parent than to see your child suffering and not be able to make it stop or to change the situation. Everything looks hopeless, no matter what you try.

> *Only in the dark can you see the stars.*
> *– Civil rights leader Martin Luther King Jr.*

The feeling that you are powerless, or that nothing you can do will make any difference, can lead you straight to suffering the other nuclear side effects we've been talking about.

The truth is that you are <u>not</u> powerless and there is <u>always</u> hope. Parents who step up to the plate and become their child's champion make an enormous difference in that child's life. You are their rock star, protector, source of love and fountain of light.

Remember, you may not <u>find</u> hope in yourself right now, but your child always <u>sees</u> hope in you.

SHAME / EMBARRASSMENT

It's hard enough raising a child with special needs without the whole world staring, passing judgments and making comments. Parents tell me how self-conscious or anxious they are about taking their child out in public, or having strangers to their home.

> *One of the reasons we judge each other so harshly in this world of parenting is because ... we perceive anyone else who's doing anything differently than what we're doing as criticizing our choices.*
> *– Researcher & educator Brené Brown*

But, the bottom line is that a child with autism often looks and behaves differently, and that <u>will</u> attract attention. If people lack understanding or sensitivity, <u>they</u> are the ones in the wrong, not you!

There's no such thing as a perfect child. Every child has "issues," some we can see, others we can't.

Remember that your child cannot control their inappropriate behavior, any more than a child with one leg can stop limping. And just because <u>you</u> can't change that, it doesn't mean that you are a horrible person or a bad parent.

> *Resentment is like taking poison and waiting for the other person to die.*
> – Actress & writer Carrie Fisher

Loving your children and doing your best for them makes you a good parent, whether your child has autism or not. Continuing to do your best in difficult circumstances makes you both a good parent and a good person.

ENVY

Why do some people who are irresponsible, insensitive, unfit and just plain horrible parents have children in perfect health with normal development?

It's hard not to resent those people, or even average parents who take their children's lack of disabilities for granted. But it's not their fault they have healthy kids, any more than it is your fault that your child has autism.

> *I learned that courage is not the absence of fear, but the triumph over it. The brave man is not one who feels no fear, but one who feels fear and conquers it.*
> – South African President Nelson Mandela

These are the hands we have been dealt – some are easier to handle than others, but nobody gets the cards they expected.

FEAR

When your child has autism, you wonder what will happen to them – in the short and long term. School, adolescence and adulthood may all look like mountains in your path. The more uncertain the future seems, the more likely you are to fear it.

All parents tend to feel anxious about their children for one reason or another. Any parent who is always totally calm about their child's future obviously hasn't been thinking about it enough!

Just like every other father or mother out there, you can't say for certain what your child's future holds. Unlike other parents, you will have to plan more carefully, over a longer term, and be even more prepared to handle the unexpected with flexibility and calm.

YOUR TRIGGERS – What Sets Off Nuclear Side Effects

What will trigger nuclear side effects? The simple answer is being human and experiencing everyday life.

A parent of a child with autism doesn't stop living and functioning in the real world. You still have to go to work and deal with bosses, co-workers, commuting and stress. You still have to go shopping, get your car repaired, cook dinner and mow the lawn.

Even in the face of something as difficult as autism, life goes on.

But your responsibilities have changed significantly. So, in addition to all of the activities and responsibilities of any parent, there are now therapists' appointments, medical appointments, extra hours for meeting your child's physical needs, research into educational programs … the list goes on and on.

In other words, you have <u>much</u> more to deal with than the average parent. And, in today's fast-moving world that can put you under a lot of stress.

> *Life is difficult for everyone. We all have stress and we all need someone in our lives that we can lean on. Never think that you cannot talk to someone because they have problems too, or that your friend or loved one would be better off without you or your problems. You'll soon find out that they need you just as much as you need them.*
> – Author, soldier & peace officer Josh Hartzell

When a person is stressed, it may not take much to set off a nuclear side effect –

- **Your child has a meltdown in public and people are staring, whispering and saying hurtful things**
- **You need to leave work 30 minutes early for an appointment, but your boss demands you stay and finish an important project**
- **A friend's baby begins saying little words, while your five-year-old can only make unpleasant noises**

Knowing which kinds of triggers are the most disturbing for you may allow you to work around them or avoid the specific situations.

We can't always avoid these triggers and we can't always react well in the heat and stress of the moment. In those cases, all we can do is apologize and try to do better in the future.

YOUR OWN DIAGNOSIS – Autism Parents' Spectrum Disorder

The experts will tell you that your child falls somewhere on the Autism Spectrum. Well, I'm here to tell you that you're also on a spectrum – you're suffering from what I call <u>Autism Parents' Spectrum Disorder</u>!

Our spectrum is made up of the five stages of grief and the various nuclear side effects we looked at in the last several pages.

All parents in our situation live somewhere on this spectrum … between coping well and struggling, between denial and Acceptance, and between hope and despair. In other words, it represents our **Journey with Autism.**

And, unlike the limited range your child has on his or her spectrum, you will go up and down, and back and forth on your spectrum, all of the time.

Dealing with all of these issues (on top of every other aspect of your life!) may make you feel as if you're trying to climb a mountain every day.

But here's the good news – the mountain <u>does</u> have a top, and you <u>can</u> climb it.

YOU'RE A CONTESTANT ON AUTISM SURVIVOR!

Congratulations! You didn't ask for it, didn't want it and had no time to prepare, but you've been selected to star in the new season of Autism Survivor.

You've been taken by helicopter and dropped in the middle of the uncharted Denial Forest. It's a confusing and dangerous environment, so get through it as quickly as you can!

In the middle of the Forest is the peak of Autism Mountain. If you can make it all the way to the top, you win the competition.

At the top of Autism Mountain is your prize – the paradise called "Acceptance". The long and difficult climb will be over. You will be able to relax, take it easy and reclaim your life. And the view will change your outlook on everything!

It's not going to be a painless journey. You could slip and fall, or slide backwards, at any time. Expect some scratches, bumps and bruises along the way.

How fast you climb the mountain, and which route you take to the top, are up to you. There are plenty of paths, up through Anger Valley, across the Envy Glacier, around Confusion Peak and lots more. You will probably end up spending time on all of them.

One thing you should know ... <u>everyone</u> who has ever climbed Autism Mountain has fallen more than once. Sometimes they even skid off the top and have to climb part of the way back up again.

But that's okay. It doesn't matter if you fall, slip or even collapse now and then.

As long as you get up again and keep climbing!

Here's what Autism Mountain looks like (at least, in my head!).

We all have to climb it to get to that peak of Acceptance. So, set your own pace and remember it's a long journey. It may take months or even years.

If you find yourself stuck on Fear Crest, or visiting the Gulley of Guilt for the third time, don't despair. There is no right or wrong way to climb the mountain – you just need to find the path that works for you.

As long as you get up every time you fall, take a couple of deep breaths and keep climbing, you will make it.

The View From the Top

Is all this really worth it? Well, here's what it feels like when you reach Acceptance –

For one thing, you will feel that you actually have some control over your life and the whole autism challenge. You will feel good about how you're handling things now, and more confident about dealing with the future.

> *Breathe. Let go. And remind yourself that this very moment is the only one you know you have for sure.* – Media star & philanthropist Oprah Winfrey

You'll be able to appreciate the positive changes in your life – the increased strength, compassion, personal growth and new friends.

Acceptance isn't about "being happy" – you will still hate the situation. The world won't be perfect, and you and your family will still be who you are. Autism won't magically stop being a problem, but you will be able to accept, adapt and thrive.

Acceptance means being realistic about today, being ready for tomorrow, and being hopeful about the future. It means believing in yourself and your family, knowing that you can handle whatever life throws at you.

Above all, Acceptance means:

- **You can look at your child and see a <u>person</u>, not a disability**

- **You can truly <u>love</u> a child who may never be "normal"**

- **You can <u>embrace</u> a life that you didn't dream about or plan for**

- **You can move on, <u>reclaim your life</u> and build a better future**

Yes, the view from the top of Autism Mountain is pretty spectacular!

You're Some Kind of Hero!

Climbing this mountain is not like running a normal marathon. You can't get it done in a few hours and there is no set route to the finish line.

And, unlike marathon runners, you have not had months or years to train. Marathoners get to prepare both physically and mentally for the challenges ahead so they can have the run of their lives.

Parents of autistic children have none of this. No one ever prepared us for the "run of our lives".

> *People who go to work every day, make sacrifices to raise families, and get through life without hurting other people if they can help it - those are the real heroes. – Author Dean Koontz*

They give people medals for climbing Mount Everest. Climbing Autism Mountain and reaching the peak of Acceptance is its own reward.

But, to all of us who have been in your shoes and struggled up the mountain, you <u>will</u> be a hero. Whenever you look up, you will see us. We're the ones cheering you on.

PART 2

HOW TO ADAPT TO YOUR NEW LIFE

WHAT NOW? – Addressing Your New Reality

Now that we've talked about all of the difficulties you're facing and all of the hard things you may go through, there's one big question to answer – what can you do about it?

The answer is "plenty"!

This section of the book is designed to give you the information, understanding and tools you need to successfully adapt to your new life.

> *Because minds do blow and hearts do break. Those are not just sayings. And wolves are not the only creatures that chew off their legs to get out of traps— human beings do that, too.*
> – Psychologist & writer Robin Silverman

Will it be easy? Probably not.

As we saw in the last section, it can take months or years to climb Autism Mountain, and there will be plenty of falls, bruises and backsliding along the way.

But it's vitally important that you take on this challenge, however many stages you need to go through, however many times you have to go through them, or whatever pace you do it at.

There are a few good reasons why:

You Can't Hide From Yourself

The grief stages and nuclear side effects are happening to you, in your heart and mind, and there's no way to hide from yourself.

You might be able to evade events or situations when they are external, but you can't do it when they are internal. Wherever you may go, there you are.

> *You cannot protect yourself from sadness without protecting yourself from happiness.*
> – Novelist & poet Jonathan Safran Foer

So, if you can't run away or hide, your only choices are to face reality and learn to cope with it, or give up. You either deal with the thoughts and feelings you are having, or let them take over your life.

People Under Pressure Can Explode

If you do try to hide from your own thoughts and feelings, you are risking some serious consequences.

Keep filling a balloon for too long and it will go off like an explosion. People are like balloons; there's only so much pressure we can handle before something gives out. Parents may experience:

- **Physical symptoms, from headaches to heart attacks**

- **Emotional symptoms, from anxiety to depression**

- **Behavioral changes, from alcohol/drug abuse to becoming verbally or physically abusive**

Using alcohol or drugs to numb yourself may feel like it's working in the short term, but substance abuse doesn't make problems go away. It only adds new problems to your life.

The longer we try to keep things bottled up, the higher the pressure goes ... and the worse it is when things finally fall apart. It's much better to deal with things as they're happening.

Managing the Process Actually Helps

Going through the stages of grief and the nuclear side effects is never easy or nice, but knowingly allowing yourself to experience them actually does help.

> *Folks are usually about as happy as they make their minds up to be.*
> – President Abraham Lincoln

It's like going through all of the steps of a medical procedure, from diagnosis to tests, surgery, recovery and rehabilitation. You will get back on your feet faster and recover more completely if you proactively take part in the process.

Many people find that the grief stages and nuclear side effects provide a framework for managing their thoughts and feelings. You have to process a huge amount of information with your heart and mind – being able to experience and label it in an "orderly" way often makes it easier.

Using the knowledge of what's happening to you will give you a greater sense of control and more confidence in your ability to take on the challenges of life with a special needs child.

A Silver Lining? Really?

If you told me 18 years ago that having a child with autism would turn out to be a remarkable experience and make me a better person, I'm not sure if I would have laughed, cried or wanted to slap you! Knowing me, probably all three.

When you're still struggling to get to Acceptance, the idea of finding a silver lining in the cloud of autism can seem ridiculous or even insulting.

> *Let the trials in your life guide you, not define you.*
> – Canadian author Kim Cormack

But those of us who have been through the process can tell you, it's true. Along with the challenges autism brings, your new reality offers you incredible opportunities for personal and spiritual growth. As the old saying goes, "what doesn't kill you makes you stronger."

There is absolutely no doubt that I am a stronger, more compassionate, confident and able person because of my family's journey. I appreciate life much more and keep things in perspective. I have a deeper understanding of myself and the world around me.

23

Yes, these lessons were learned the hard way – nobody is going to <u>choose</u> self-improvement through autism! – but I can honestly say becoming the person I am today has been worth it.

Going through your own version of the ups and downs of the grief stages and nuclear side effects is actually a healthy part of adjusting to your new reality.

FAMILY IMPACTS – How Autism Affects Everyone

Autism doesn't happen in a vacuum. It touches everyone around the affected child, particularly the family. In order for you to reclaim your life, you need to be aware of (and handle!) the impact of autism on your loved ones.

You, your partner and other family members may end up taking different routes up Autism Mountain, reaching different stages at different times, with each getting to Acceptance at their own pace.

That can be hard to accept – for you and the others around you. It can be frustrating trying to communicate with someone in a different stage than yours, or who is struggling with a challenge you've already overcome.

You see, in every story, it's not about the ending. It's about the chapters in between and how you make it through them. – Actress & writer Courtney Giardina

Because other family members are probably not as severely affected as you, the parent, you may see them whizzing through stages you wrestled with for months. Or you may find yourself getting impatient with a grandfather or sister who seems to be having a harder time than you.

Remember – there is no right or wrong way to climb the mountain. Everyone has to find their own path at their own pace. So, try to be as patient with others as you would like them to be understanding of you.

Just like you can hate the diagnosis but love your child, you can also hate the <u>stage</u> someone is going through but still love the <u>person</u>.

If you can keep the grief stage or nuclear side effect separate from the person you love, you will improve your relationship and help prevent long-term barriers from forming.

You & Your Partner

Many marriages would be much improved if the husband and wife clearly understood that they are on the same side. – Motivational speaker Zig Ziglar

The two of you are going to be raising your child, so you need to work on being on the same page, being supportive and working together as much as possible.

I'm not saying this is easy. Not only are <u>you</u> reacting to the autism diagnosis, the grief stages and nuclear side effects, but your partner is too. And this is hard for both of you.

Step back and look at the situation -- you have two people in a major crisis at the same time, and each of them may be reacting in totally different and unpredictable ways. Is it any wonder that common ground may be hard to find?

This can lead to what seems like an impossible situation because neither you nor your partner is "yourself" at all. Your true personality can be buried under the stress of the situation.

Typically, in a crisis, one parent remains level-headed, calm and strong while the other goes through emotional turmoil. They may stay in these roles or change places over time. Either way, it's an uncertain and frustrating situation.

It's important to take the time to assess where you both are on the autism parents' spectrum. For example, you may move quickly to Acceptance and take proactive steps to help your child while your partner may be stuck in denial and doesn't want to hear anything about autism.

Understanding what grief stage your partner is in, or which nuclear side effect he/she is experiencing, can help you better understand his or her thinking and behavior.

And it is important to step back and do the same assessment for yourself occasionally as well to see where you're at.

Keep in mind that both of your emotions and behaviors will be up and down or "all-over-the-place" while going through the grief stages or reacting to the nuclear side effects. But there are many things you can do to help each other:

- **Check in with each other frequently to ask "How's it going" or "How are you feeling".**

- **Tell each other things like "This is really hard for me" or "I can't handle this one".**

- **Provide a safe haven for each other, where you can vent out or cry about the situation. There's no shame in showing each other how you really truly feel.**

- **Don't feel compelled to wear that "brave" face with each other. It's exhausting enough showing it to everyone around you.**

- **Show love, compassion and support to each other. A reassuring hug or supportive telephone call or text can go a long way when you're feeling down and out, or lost and confused.**

More importantly, try not to take things too personally. Most of your partner's negative emotions or behavior isn't really being directed at you, but rather at the situation. Little things can start to bother or upset you. So when your partner gets angry about the dishes not being placed in the dishwasher properly, and this was never an issue before, it's probably just anger at the situation coming out.

> *Kindness is a currency that can cover a multitude of interpersonal debts.* – Inspirational writer George Alexiou

It may be hard for you to see or know the difference between personal and situational anger in the early days or months following the diagnosis. Talking with each other regularly and honestly can help solve the little misunderstandings that occur in all relationships from time to time.

Remember, it's easier to put out a little spark than a full-fledged fire.

You & Your Partner – The Love Factor

Always remember, your partner loves you. There may be times when it doesn't feel that way, or you feel that you don't know your partner anymore. There may be times when you feel like your relationship is falling apart, and you start fearing a possible future without your partner.

Just keep in mind that these are temporary stages that your relationship is going through because of the new and unexpected stresses of dealing with autism in your lives. It doesn't mean you have a bad relationship or that you're going to break up. All relationships get tested at some point, so autism will be your test.

As hard as it may be, you have to allow your partner the time to go through the grief stages and experience the nuclear side effects; time to suffer and to heal. Your partner has to do the same for you.

You're both going to need a lot of patience and understanding, and they may be in short supply at times, especially when you have your own pain to deal with.

> *Patience may be bitter, but its fruit is sweet. – Ancient Greek philosopher Aristotle*

But you can do it and it will be worth it.

Be patient and compassionate with each other. Acceptance and healing doesn't happen overnight, so cut each other some slack; you're only human.

Go ahead and hate the diagnosis. Hate the situation you're in and the impact it's having on your relationship. Just as long as you remember to keep loving and supporting one another.

Try to keep things in perspective. This may be a difficult time in your marriage, but you can emerge stronger and more united from it.

And it may not seem like it now, but there will come a day when you'll both be on the same page when it comes to your child. And what a beautiful day that will be!

You & Your Family - Pulling Together For The Common Good

Communication and teamwork -- these are the key words when it comes to helping yourself and your family adapt to your new reality.

You have to be able to communicate with each other, even about negative thoughts and feelings. In some cases, this is harder for men than for women, although I've seen plenty of examples where the opposite is also true.

It can help to develop your own language to describe what's happening and little signals you can give each other when you're having difficulty. This will help you be more aware of how everyone in your family, including you, is handling things.

> *Teamwork is the fuel that allows common people to achieve uncommon results. –*
> Business legend & philanthropist
> Andrew Carnegie

It also helps create a feeling of teamwork, and that's vital.

You, your partner and other family members have to agree that, whatever else is happening and however much you may frustrate or annoy each other, you all have a job to do – <u>together.</u>

Whatever strengths or weaknesses your family has, you are all stronger working together than any one of you can be individually. Teamwork makes the impossible possible.

You Call This A Team?

When I talk to parents of children with autism about the idea of their family becoming a team, many of them say things like, "<u>My</u> family? Are you kidding?"

If you're thinking the same thing, don't dismiss the idea just because your family members seem to be unlikely team-mates. The people who love you <u>want</u> to help you, but may not know the best way to do it.

They all share a <u>powerful</u> common interest in your child.

The biggest problem is that members of your family are probably scattered all over Autism Mountain or even still trapped in the Forest of Denial. They're all dealing with their individual grief stages and nuclear side effects.

So, you may be facing a situation like this:

- **Grandma Rose says there's nothing wrong with your child and she should know; she raised five kids. Those doctors don't know anything, she tells you, just ignore that nonsense.**

- **Older brother Kyle is fed up because so much of your time and attention goes to the child with autism, and there's no money for a new bike because his sibling needs more therapy.**

- **Uncle Ed is feeling guilty because all of <u>his</u> kids are healthy, but his sister has to go through so much with <u>her</u> child. It makes him feel so bad that he hardly ever visits anymore.**

- Cousin Miriam read about a doctor who put a child with autism on a banana and veal chop diet and it "cured" that girl in one month flat. Isn't his $1 million fee worth it?

You call <u>this</u> a team? Well, not yet. It's more like this:

AUTISM FAMILY BUMPER CARS

You and your family are at the amusement park and ready to go on the Autism Family Bumper Car ride.

Mom and Dad get into their red bumper car with a sticker on the side that says ACCEPTANCE.

Oh-oh, here comes Grandma in her big pink DENIAL bumper car! She's headed straight for Uncle Ed's yellow GUILT car at top speed.

Over in the corner, big brother Kyle is revving up his green RESENTMENT car and glaring at Mom and Dad, while cousin Miriam is getting in everyone's way with her purple DESPERATION bumper car.

Soon there are collisions everywhere – people losing control and heading in all directions. It's chaos!

If this sounds like your family, then it's time for an intervention ...

HELPING YOURSELVES – Family Summits

I have seen some incredible family teams going to bat for a child with autism, handling challenges together, cheering each other on, supporting their team-mates through hard times, and generally making each other's lives better.

Being a part of "Team Tracy" or "Team Adrian" gives everyone a clear role to play, so they all know they are contributing to the well-being of you and your child. It helps keep everyone on the same page, so there are fewer arguments and misunderstandings. And teamwork can bring people together in a positive, productive atmosphere that really makes a difference.

A successful family wins as a team. But if its members are intent upon winning their own individual battles with one another, the team loses.
– Inspirational e-zine publisher Steve Goodier

Okay, so how do we get from Family Bumper Cars Madness to this elite Super-squad? You build the team, person by person, through family summits.

Start Small

The first step may be just a mini-summit between you and your partner, who are the co-leaders or co-captains of the family team. You have to be prepared to put your individual issues aside and decide to cooperate for the greater good – the common goal of doing the best for your child.

> *Every great dream begins with a dreamer. Always remember, you have within you the strength, the patience, and the passion to reach for the stars to change the world.*
> – Anti-slavery activist Harriet Tubman

That's going to require some give and take, and probably some "we agree to disagree" moments as well. With strong emotions and your child's welfare involved, it may be difficult to have a calm and productive discussion. If it doesn't work on the first attempt, try again another time. Remember, Rome wasn't built in a day.

Once you and your partner agree on how you will operate as team captains, and decide on the major issues and/or concerns you want to address with your family, you can start bringing in individual team members, one at a time.

You want to get each family member on board by acknowledging the grief stage or nuclear side effect they're in and showing them how they can use their love, energy and expertise to benefit your child.

You've probably dedicated a lot of time and effort to educating yourself. Now you can help to educate the other important people involved in your child's life.

Share what you've learned about autism, and yes, that includes the "good, bad, and ugly". Your family members will appreciate and probably sympathize with what you've been dealing with because, prior to this, they've only seen your "brave and/or strong" face. They will definitely want to help you, so show them how they can be part of your child's team.

Growing slowly, in phases, your team will have to learn to handle differing opinions and needs. With a bit of patience and good will from everyone involved, you can usually make things work. But there will be times when you will have to let certain issues go and not discuss them anymore – not everyone is ready for all situations or information.

It may take weeks or months, but when you bring the whole team together and focus your efforts to help your child, you will be amazed at what you can accomplish!

Your family team is going to be very similar to a team in sports or business. Keep everyone informed about what the objectives are and what role each member is playing, because they will continue to change over time. Send out brief updates via telephone, text or e-mail so everyone knows how your child is doing. You need to celebrate your victories together but also review your setbacks together and learn to do better next time.

All the rules of good teamwork apply to your squad, from putting the team first to respecting your team-mates and keeping your eye on the goal.

And be sure to thank your family for their support regularly. Always let them know how much you appreciate everything they are doing.

Some May Not Play Well With Others

Not everyone is going to make the team.

Some people are just not cut out for cooperating with a group. Others may be stuck in a stage or nuclear side effect that is blocking them from participating.

> *Never try to teach a pig to sing – it wastes your time and annoys the pig.*
> – Humorist & author Mark Twain

You may end up with some cheerleaders who don't actually contribute directly to the team, but offer support and encouragement from the sidelines.

And, sometimes, the best you can do is to get people to stop playing <u>against</u> you!

Remember that, even though they are not the parents and cannot feel the challenges as strongly as you do, other members of your family are still being affected. They're coming from the same places as you – love, concern, empathy and a desire to help.

LIFE TOGETHER – You and Your Child

So far, we've been talking about how life in the world of autism and all of the shock waves and side effects it creates can affect you and others around you.

Now, it's time to bring it back to the most important relationship of all – the one between you and your child.

Spectrum Meets Spectrum

I'm not going to try to tell you how to raise your child, how to handle their autism issues or anything else that is covered in the thousands of other books on the market. Every parent's child and situation is unique.

The only point I want to make here is this: <u>everything you're going through affects your child</u>.

All of the grief stages and nuclear side effects that impact you send ripples out that touch your child.

> *Strength does not come from winning. Your struggles develop your strengths. When you go through hardships and decide not to surrender, <u>that</u> is strength.* – Actor & politician Arnold Schwarzenegger

You may be surprised to know that your stress, depression and other negative states can be picked up by your child; if you are distracted or impatient, and something else is "wrong", your child can certainly sense it.

In other words, your child is right there with you, experiencing all the same things as you.

Just as you are directly affected by your child's autism spectrum, he or she is affected by your Autism Parents' Spectrum Disorder.

These two spectrums don't exist independent of each other – **they're intertwined**. You and your child will experience them together for as long as your lives touch.

Fasten Your Seatbelts & Lose Your Baggage

It has taken me many years to understand how much the child and parent spectrums interact with each other and to start taking this into account in our lives.

I think of it like this:

IT'S GOING TO BE A BUMPY FLIGHT!

Ladies and gentlemen, welcome aboard Autism Airways, Flight 101. We'll be making several unscheduled stops on our way to our final destination and our flight time is unknown.

Before taking off, we ask that you pay attention to this important safety demonstration:

Please make sure that your seat belt is securely fastened at all times, even when you think you're okay. Parents should fasten their safety belts first and then ensure that your child's safety belt is properly fastened.

In the very likely event of an emergency, oxygen masks will drop from the ceiling above your seat. If you are traveling with a child, it's important to put your mask on first and then place the other mask on your child. You have to be prepared to help your child immediately.

Finally, the captain advises that we are going to be passing through a number of levels of turbulence on this flight, including Anger, Guilt and Bargaining.

Even after we achieve our cruising height of Acceptance, where skies are clear, please be aware that unexpected air pockets such as Shame and Hopelessness, may cause us to lose altitude rapidly and we'll have to climb through the turbulence all over again.

Once again, thank you for joining us on Autism Airways (not that you had much choice).

Now, hang on everybody – it's going to be a bumpy flight!

So, there are going to be plenty of thunderstorms, winds and other unexpected "acts of nature" on this flight.

The worst is when you're up there at Acceptance, among the fluffy white clouds and sunshine, and an air pocket drops you ten thousand feet in no time flat!

There may be times when you are sure the plane is going to crash, or that you are going to be sick because of all the ups and downs.

But when you turn to your child, you <u>must</u> be the picture of calmness. No anxiety or fear shows on your face, and your voice is full of confidence.

If you need to scream or throw up, do it in the bathroom and not in front of your child. By staying calm in front of him or her, you offer reassurance and a model of how to react to life's turbulence.

By the way, you'll find this a whole lot easier if you leave as much of your emotional baggage behind as possible. Don't add the extra weight of the autism burden to an already difficult flight – travel as light and easy as you can.

MANAGING EXPECTATIONS – Be Positive but Realistic

I'm sure that NBA star Kobe Bryant, at 6'6" tall, would not be very good as a horse racing jockey. And I'm pretty confident that I will never win the Nobel Prize for physics or become a professional opera singer.

I'm not being negative, just realistic. Every person and every life has limitations.

This is an important, but difficult, lesson for parents of children with autism.

Having unrealistic expectations about your child will only lead to stress and disappointment. You must still be positive about the future, but keep your expectations grounded in reality.

That applies to you, as a parent, as well. Try to have realistic expectations of yourself, particularly in the early years when you are still on the autism learning curve.

Getting Real

First things first: Parenting is a hard job. Period.

> *Keep calm and carry on.*
> – British slogan during World War II

Think back to when you used to get on your parents' nerves and they would smile at you and say "You'll see. Just wait till you have your own kids". Well, they were right, weren't they?

Now in our case, it is most definitely harder than for the average parent. We have to deal with a ton of things that parents of typically developing children don't have to. But I think the most important thing we can do is to be a parent **first**, and then a parent of a child with autism, second. **And that is a very important mental shift we have to make in our minds.** Because, sometimes, we can be our own worst enemies.

We have to <u>stop defining ourselves</u> by the autism. We begin to think that we're just "the parent of that kid with autism" and our parenting self-identity changes. Are we any less a parent because we have a child with autism? Do we love our children less than parents of typical children? Of course not.

Then why do we make ourselves feel less worthy? Again, you have to remember -- you're not to blame for your child's autism. No one is.

The **second**, most difficult mindset change you'll have to make is this:

LOVE YOUR CHILD   HATE THE DIAGNOSIS

AND LEARN HOW TO TELL THE DIFFERENCE

One of the toughest things about raising a child with autism is the behaviors it causes in your child. While each child with autism develops and behaves differently, it's pretty likely that your child will exhibit a few behaviors that may make you feel frustrated or embarrassed. Depending on where your child falls on the autism spectrum, that list of behaviors might include:

- **Rocking in place, maybe for hours with no break**

- **Head twirling in an endless circle or talking to hands**

- **Making odd sounds – bird-like chirps or monkey-like grunts**

- **Banging their head against a wall or other surface**

- **Refusing to eat if plates and utensils are not placed in a particular order or a color of a vegetable is the wrong "shade" of that color**

- **Obsessing over a particular issue, such as wearing a certain color or outfit all the time or refusing to play with toys if they are not lined up in a specific order**

Should you hate the autism that makes your child do these things? Absolutely! Hate the diagnosis with a capital <u>**H!**</u> Just don't mix up the diagnosis with the person.

It helps to remind yourself that these behaviors are <u>not</u> choices; they are the result of a neurological disorder. Just like diabetes prevents a person's body from responding properly to blood sugar changes, <u>autism stops your child's brain from reacting "normally" to stimulation.</u>

Our natural way of looking at things is to put a person and his or her behavior together. You can't do that with disorders like autism – the two things are separate.

As difficult as it may be to absorb this concept, **this is one of the first and most critical steps to successfully raising a child with autism.**

Will this happen overnight? Obviously not! But, in time, you will start to focus less on your child's behavior and more on your child. And eventually, you'll begin to **see** your child and look past or even ignore the behaviors he or she is exhibiting.

When you learn how to do that, wonderful and exciting things begin to happen:

- **You'll start to see that your child is a "diamond in the making", full of possibility.**

- **When you look at your child, you won't be filled with despair anymore; you'll be filled with hope because, now, you see the potential in your child.**

- **You can focus on the little things that your child does well, and not only those things he or she does poorly.**

- **You can see your child's unique personality blossom and realize that each child is a gift.**

- **And you'll realize that you can raise your child to be the best person he or she can be, just like any other parent.**

Remember, your child will change as he or she gets older. No one stays the same forever. Your child may reduce or even outgrow these behaviors as time goes on. And there are always doctors, therapists and other professionals who can work with you to help address these behaviors.

Don't allow these autistic behaviors to prevent you from loving and developing a close relationship with your child. And don't **define** your child by them either. We make allowances for other people in our life whose behaviors annoy us, so we have to do the same for our children.

Let's face it; we all have family and friends who drive us crazy with their behaviors. There's the friend who smacks his gum so loud while chewing. There's your relative who twirls her hair every five seconds when talking to you, which drives you insane. The list can go on and on.

The point is that people may have behaviors that are annoying, but that doesn't stop you from loving them or them loving you.

You have to process and accept that your child is <u>innocent</u>. He or she didn't ask to be born with autism, but is just a victim of circumstance. It is no one's fault. It just is.

Just remember that your child and the diagnosis are two different things – one deserves your hate and the other needs all of your love.

There's no benchmark for how life's "supposed" to happen. There is no ideal world for you to wait around for. The world is always just what it is now; it's up to you how you respond to it.
– Novelist Isaac Marion

What You Can and Can't Do

As I said earlier on, your child can't help exhibiting the traits of autism any more than a child with one leg can help limping.

And the fact that you can't make their behavior instantly stop does not mean you are a failure as a parent. Most parents of special needs children struggle with this aspect of autism. So, you're in good company and definitely not alone.

Again, this is about being positive but realistic in how you manage your expectations.

There are certain things that you simply <u>can't</u> do –

- **"Cure" your child**

- **Stop people from looking**

- **Make your child "behave normally"**

- **Be perfect, strong, positive, patient, understanding and brave 100% of the time**

The good news is that the list of things you <u>can</u> do is much longer!

- **Recognize that your child's behaviors are symptoms of autism. Your child is not doing this on purpose and cannot "choose" to control it.**

- **Put yourself in your child's place. How would you feel if you couldn't speak or communicate your needs and wants? Wouldn't you want to lash out at something or someone?**

- **Manage your reactions to situations and behaviors that you can't control.**

- **Develop a thick skin. Know that people will talk and they will stare. Resist the urge to punch everyone who looks at your kid funny!**

- **Educate the public. Bystanders may not know your child is autistic. Unless they're using a wheelchair or other adaptive equipment, people may not think your child has a disability.**

- **Become a detective; use clues and common sense to figure out what may be triggering your child's behaviors and symptoms.**

- **Remember that you and your child are both on a spectrum; both of your behaviors affect the other person. You're connected to each other.**

- **Accept your new role. Be determined to do the best job you can, but cut yourself slack if you sometimes fall short of your own standards or goals.**

This list could go on and on because you are the most important factor in your child's life. Every time you take a positive mindset, you help yourself <u>and</u> your child.

Some of the "can do" items on this list can make a huge difference in the quality of life for both of you, so let's take a closer look at them ...

<u>You Can Deal With People Who Stare</u>

You can politely tell bystanders that your child has autism and becomes fearful or anxious in public. That is why he/she behaves that way. Most people will understand and give you a "sympathetic smile" and sheepishly apologize for staring at your child.

> *We all make choices, but in the end our choices make us.*
> — TV producer and writer Ken Levine

The signs of autism are not always obvious, especially for people who have never dealt with a disability. So, those impolite bystanders may honestly think your child is just behaving badly for no good reason.

Instead of getting angry about people's ignorance, use your child's autism in a positive way to educate. Just think, you can be a living "public service announcement" in your community.

And don't forget that virtually every parent has had strangers wonder about their child at some point. I know a couple with a daughter who was diagnosed with the inattentive form of ADHD and spent her toddler years in a dream world, talking to herself while playing with spoons and string.

You can bet those parents heard a lot of whispers and endured a lot of strange looks! (By the way, that girl is now on the Honors List in high school.) All children do odd things, each is different from the next kid, and every one of them deserves to be labelled "special".

You Can Recognize Your Own Meltdowns

That's right, your meltdowns.

Adults don't like to admit it and we use different words to rationalize our behavior. You might say that you lost your temper or blew your cool. People often tell themselves they just had a bad moment and usually handle things better than that.

But the truth is that **we autism parents have meltdowns**, just like our kids do. So, we have to learn to better manage our reactions to situations that we can't control. Both adult and child exhibit symptoms that reflect their spectrums. Both kinds of meltdowns need the same kind of patient understanding in response.

> *Sometimes it takes a meltdown to cool down.*
> — Inspirational writer Evinda Lepins

You Can See Things From The Other Side

Your child is trapped in his or her mind and/or body by autism. Special needs children may have to deal with frustration, fear and anxiety in a world that doesn't always make sense to them.

And yes, there will probably be times when you feel trapped as well, in a life that you didn't expect. But you can walk away now and again – your child can't. You can communicate and deal with your feelings

> *The three key factors to achieving anything worthwhile are – one, hard work; two, perseverance; and three, common sense.*
> — Inventor Thomas Edison

better than any child, particularly one with autism.

So, see it from your child's point of view as they look to you for comfort, protection and love.

You Can Use Common Sense

There are plenty of things that medical experts can tell you about autistic behavior and caring for your child. But there is also common sense. And many times, because we are so focused on the "autism", we lose sight of that.

A child who is hitting his or her stomach and screaming may simply be constipated or have an upset stomach. A child who is irritable may simply be in need of more sleep. A child who has a mini-meltdown at school may simply be hungry because it takes an hour for the teaching staff to get everyone off the bus and in for breakfast.

Don't overlook the obvious or always think of a complex autism-related reason for your child's behavior. **Sometimes kids with autism have the same childhood problems as other kids.**

Common sense and a parent's gut instinct can take you a long way!

You Can Become A Detective

The life of a child with autism can be a mystery to parents; the best way to solve a mystery is to do what smart detectives do – gather evidence and look for clues!

A good autism detective looks at a child's <u>entire</u> routine from morning to night. That means keeping a journal or writing things down on your computer to establish patterns of behavior, and tracking which events, incidents or activities trigger certain behaviors. It's also helpful to take photos or jot down notes on your cell phone as behaviors are occurring so you won't forget.

That evidence will give you the clues to what is going on in your child's mind. Then, you may be able to modify your child's behavior by changing those factors you have tracked down.

You Can Accept Your New Role

In addition to being a parent, there are a host of new roles that having a child with autism will make you take on, whether you like it or not. And, take it from me, you probably won't like it much, especially in the beginning.

> *Trust yourself. You know more than you think you do.*
> *– Parenting specialist*
> Dr. Benjamin Spock

These may be some of the times that nuclear side effects appear in full force. Blame and resentment are two that may figure prominently.

- **You are now "caregiver in chief". This means that you may be taking care of your child's personal needs (i.e., toileting, feeding, bathing, etc.) way past the infant/ toddler stage. In some cases, this may carry into the teenage and adult years.**

- **You are now the in-house therapist. You will have to learn about occupational, speech and physical therapy for your child, if your child requires one or all of them. You will** have to learn new terms like "sensory integration" and "applied behavior analysis" or ABA for short.

- **You will get a crash course and on-the-job training in the world of special education and/or special needs. It is probably a career change you hadn't planned on!**

Some parents will embrace these roles without resistance because it will help their child. Others may hate these new responsibilities and avoid them like the plague. Many will perform their duties but complain the whole time.

And then there are some parents who truly don't have the ability to handle these roles. Parenting in general is difficult for them so raising a child with special needs is just too overwhelming.

We shouldn't judge these parents, or ourselves, as "weak". As I said, every person and every life has limitations.

It really depends on the individuals and where they are on the autism parents' spectrum. The more a parent can accept and adapt, the easier their life will be.

<u>You Can Forgive Yourself</u>

You know that taking on the additional responsibilities of a special needs child is not easy. So, be prepared to forgive yourself for being a mere human being and not a superhero.

You didn't sign up for this life any more than your child did. You're allowed to be upset about this. You're allowed to have moments of anger, doubt and frustration. You are allowed to fail – as long as you keep trying again, it's okay.

Again, you're human.

You're not supposed to be an overnight expert in autism or special education. Doctors, neurologists and other medical specialists spent years in medical school and in residency programs, learning what to do.

Teachers and therapists spent years in college and grad school to learn their skills. You're not a failure if you don't become an autism encyclopedia in a week.

For that matter, don't beat yourself up if you can't become an autism expert even after months of effort. It takes time to master everything while also working full time, doing your household chores, raising your child, etc.

> *The weak can never forgive. Forgiveness is an attribute of the strong.*
> — Indian leader Mahatma Ghandi

The fact that you're taking on all of these challenges at once makes you an amazing parent and a good person!

YOU ARE AN A+ PARENT – Take Pride in Your Family

So often, parents in our situation feel autism like a stigma, as if we all had to walk around wearing a huge scarlet letter 'A' on our chests. It's easy to imagine that everybody is staring at you and whispering bad things behind your back.

But parents shouldn't feel this way. In fact, they should turn that scarlet letter 'A' into a badge of honor that proudly says "**A+ Parent**".

All parents who stay and accept the challenges of raising a child with autism deserve a medal for courage. You have faced up to your responsibility, even though it means braving uncharted territory. Even though you didn't know what was ahead, you took a deep breath and walked on.

> *Heroes may not all be big and strong, smart or witty, attractive or chivalrous, or dashingly handsome. Heroes come in all different shapes and sizes, but they all have one thing in common, they have a cause, a reason to fight, a reason to live. Even if they don't know it yet.*
> – Photographer & artist Ben Lafond

Because of your courage and determination, your child will have a better life. That's something worth patting yourself on the back about!

Kicking yourself for not being a perfect parent is easy. It's also unproductive and unfair. **There are no perfect parents**, only real human beings doing the best they can.

And we have a word to describe people who live up and face up to challenges – we call them heroes. Even if the world at large doesn't recognize it, <u>you will always be a hero</u> to your child, and to all of us who have walked in your shoes.

THE FIX-IT TOUR – Answers, Not Cures

Remember the imaginary trip we took a few chapters back on Autism Airways – the up and down flight through all that turbulence?

Well, that airplane is now taking you on a journey that I call the Fix-It Tour:

THE WHEELS TOUCH DOWN

Autism Airways, Flight 101 has landed at its first stop – a strange, foreign country full of new languages, bizarre rituals and superstitions.

Somewhere here may be the help you're looking for and the answers you seek. But, where to start?

As soon as you exit the terminal, you're surrounded by a crowd of people ... taxi drivers who want to take you to hotels ... guides who want to escort you to historic attractions ... hawkers who want to sell you beads, rugs and magic elixirs.

Surrounded by noise and confusion, you're going to have to determine who to trust. Who are the scam artists and who are the honest people?

It's going to be the same story at every stop on this flight. You're on the Fix-It Tour – a trip around the world of autism, searching for a solution.

Better keep your eyes open, and one hand on your wallet or purse ...

Every parent goes on their own personal version of the Fix-It Tour. It usually starts with visits to medical specialists like pediatric neurologists, developmental delays experts, psychologists and therapists. There may be visits to hospitals or medical centers for additional tests like an MRI to determine the cause of the disability.

> *Better to know the quick pain of truth than the ongoing pain of a long-held false hope.*
> – Australian children's author Trudi Canavan

Nothing wrong with that, is there? Of course you should look into every logical possibility. Just be honest about why you are on this tour.

Are you secretly hoping that someone will tell that you that your child was misdiagnosed and this whole "autism madness" has been one huge mistake?

Are you thinking you can find someone, or some intervention/drug/therapy/diet, to "cure" your child of autism?

If so, let me save you years of heartbreak, frustration and wasted money. There is no magic pill, no secret antidote repressed by the medical community, no "cure" for autism.

There are answers out there – excellent treatments, resources and therapies that will help your child. But, however far you go, however many tour stops you make, you should not expect to find anybody or anything to eliminate your child's autism.

Yes, miracles do happen, but if you go out there expecting that one in a billion chance, you will get your heart repeatedly broken.

Exiting the Fix-It Tour

The longer you stay on the Fix-It Tour, the more bad news and false hopes you may get. Don't do this to yourself or your child.

> *I went to a bookstore and asked the saleswoman, 'Where's the self-help section?' She said if she told me, it would defeat the purpose.*
> – Comedian George Carlin

It's particularly hard for men – they are natural fixers and want to find the solution. The strength of men is that they refuse to admit defeat and keep battling, but they have to learn to turn that energy into the positive battle for getting the right help for their child.

There is a better alternative to the heartbreak of the Fix-It Tour – a realistic search for appropriate help.

Yes, you must be tireless and proactive in advocating for your child. You must be a thousand percent sure of the diagnosis – it's smart to get second and third opinions to confirm the condition.

However, your end goal must change. You can't go looking for "quick-fixes" or cures. You must realize that what you need, and what you can really find, are accurate and reliable answers and solid, professional help.

Tips For a Successful Search

Even when you manage your expectations and go looking for the best answers and treatment for your child with a realistic attitude, the search will take a lot out of you.

Here are some tips to help you make the most of your time, energy and money:

- **You need to know that you may experience roadblocks, setbacks and other disappointments along the way. You can try something you're sure will help your child, and it doesn't work. Then, you're back to square one again and looking for more people to see and things to do.**

- **Be prepared when meeting with medical experts. It makes for a more productive and effective meeting. Know your child's medical history as well as that of you and your partner. The more information you provide, the better you'll be able to help medical professionals assess your child. Also, they may use confusing medical terms, so ask them to explain things to you in everyday language.**

- **It's very important to note that most of these specialists are evaluating your child for a short period of time. Many times, they may spend an hour or less with you and your child. They may observe, ask your child to perform certain tasks to assess their skill level, etc. but they are not living with your child every day. So, it is extremely beneficial if you could provide actual examples of your child's behavior.**

  - **Use your cell phone to take pictures or videotape your child in different settings, such as your home or in public and participating in various activities.**

  - **Bring along a copy of your "detective" notes that we talked about earlier. You can offer specific examples and times of your child's behaviors because of the thorough information you have been compiling. This will give the specialist a more complete and accurate portrait of your child.**

- **Schedule a time that is good for your child. For example, making an appointment during your child's regular meal or nap time is a bad idea. He or she will be irritable because of hunger or fatigue. Shoot for a time that best suits your child. Bring a favorite toy, video or snack to make your child feel more comfortable during the appointment.**

- **Don't underestimate your child's understanding of these visits. Even though your child may not verbally communicate it to you, he or she may be nervous. They are in a new, unfamiliar setting with a bunch of strangers staring at them, asking them to perform a bunch of tasks which are unfamiliar to them. They may also be picking up on your nerves or excitement.**

- **If you've ever blown a job interview, you know how a bad case of nerves can leave you performing under your best standard. Well, the same thing can happen to your child. On the particular day, in that one hour of assessment, your child may have a nuclear meltdown with all of the specialists watching. If their diagnosis is based on that one example of behavior, is it truly accurate?**

The point is that you live with your child, 24/7. The specialists don't.

You know your child better than anyone. You see a full range of behaviors in your child, in a variety of settings. At these evaluations and meetings with specialists, they are evaluating just a moment in time or snapshot of your child in a very different environment.

Medical and autism specialists may make a diagnosis or deliver projections about your child's future, based on this evaluation, that you strongly disagree with.

I'm not saying you should ignore what the experts say. They are highly-trained and edu-cated individuals and may be seeing things you can't see, or don't want to. They're not the bad guys -- they really do want to assist you and your child. Just keep all opinions and diagnoses (including your own!) in perspective.

Also, it's important to find medical professionals and specialists who you trust and are a good "fit" for you and your family. Some doctors and experts may be direct and to the point, while others may be more talkative and personable.

> *When you take the time to actually listen, with humility, to what people have to say, it's amazing what you can learn. Especially if the people who are doing the talking also hap-pen to be children.*
> – Education activist Greg Mortenson

Use these meetings and evaluations as a screening process to find those doctors or specialists you would like to consult or stay with as your child develops and gets older.

You're a consumer, paying good money for import-ant services, so get the best that you can. You're also a champion for your child, advocating for someone who depends on your help, so don't settle for less than your child needs.

The Sad Side of the Search

Sometimes, after speaking with these doctors or experts, you may feel like giving up. If your child didn't perform as you'd hoped, you may feel that your child will never get better or have a chance for a good life.

For example, you may have a child who is five years old and the specialist tells you that your child is functioning as a ten-month-old baby. That's hard to hear and hard to bear. Believe me, I know.

But no one can say for certain where your child may truly be at six years old. Every child, including those with autism, is a bundle of possibilities and potential.

> *In a world filled with hate, we must still dare to hope. In a world filled with anger, we must still dare to comfort. In a world filled with despair, we must still dare to dream. And in a world filled with distrust, we must still dare to believe.*
> – Performer Michael Jackson

That's why you have to continue to seek professional help and treatment for your child. A child's condi-tion can change. How many times have you heard or read in the news of cases where people wake up from comas, or some other vegetative state, and begin talking, just out of the blue?

As hard as it may get, parents must never give up on their children. You must remember that no one is perfect -- doctors and specialists included. They are humans who sometimes make mistakes, just like the rest of us.

And the body of knowledge they rely on is always expanding. New research is being conducted on autism and advances, no matter how small, are being made.

The Power of Hope

You always have to have <u>hope</u>. Don't let anything or anybody take it away from you.

Never underestimate your child and what he or she may be processing. No one knows 100% how the brain works and processes information. So stimulate your child and his or her senses; good teachers and therapists can help develop activities that can be done in your home and for very little money.

Also, read and talk to your child regularly, even if it seems like he or she isn't paying attention. If possible, take your child out into the community and expose him or her to different activities and events.

Above all, while you're searching, <u>always</u> love your child. Display boatloads of affection -- hugs, kisses, rubs on the cheek. Even the most non-responsive child on the spectrum needs to receive love and may even surprise you by responding in some small but meaningful way.

> *This fire that we call Loving is too powerful for human minds. But just right for human souls.*
> – Poet and historian Aberjhani

And for those children who prefer not to be touched or held, look for ways to engage them in a way that <u>they</u> find comfortable, and sharing things or activities which they find interesting. Reaching out this way is another expression of your love for your child.

Now That You Know

So, you now know how the arrival of autism in your life is affecting yourself and your family. You also have some strategies on how to cope with those impacts.

Now, what do you do with this knowledge and these skills?

You take action!

And the final section of this book will help you create the plan for effective action; for re-taking control and reclaiming your life ...

PART 3

BUILDING YOUR AUTISM BATTLE PLAN

"CHOPPERS! I HEAR CHOPPERS!"

Another hot day in the jungle of the Autism Wilderness and confused, discouraged parents wander lost in the thick foliage.

Suddenly, a strange sound is heard from the sky – growing steadily closer and louder. People stop to look upwards in mingled fear and hope.

"Choppers! I hear choppers!" shouts a father who is a Gulf War veteran. "Could it be true", the parents talk amongst themselves, "that we are NOT alone?"

Soon hundreds of helicopters appear, hovering over the Wilderness and dropping boxes of supplies. Taped to the top of each box is a map, showing the way to the large clearing at the base of Autism Mountain.

At the bottom of the map, a message is written:

"Had enough? Ready to fight back? The Autism Army wants YOU!"

=================

Parents who follow the map are astounded to see the size of the crowd gathering in the forest clearing. There are tens of thousands of people, with more arriving every minute!

Huge signs around the clearing read "Welcome to the Autism Army!", "Let's fight back!", "Together we are strong!" and other inspiring slogans.

Every face holds a strong emotion, from defiance and determination to hope and anger. Looking around at one another, the people realize they <u>are</u> ready to fight.

They are sick and tired of having autism control their actions and take over their thinking. They've had enough of feeling trapped and limited, of guilt and frustration. They want to reclaim their lives!

But, parents ask each other, <u>how</u> do we fight and <u>where</u> do we begin?

The Gulf War vet climbs to the top of a tall rock in the middle of the clearing and raises his hands. Slowly, silence spreads across the crowd and all eyes turn toward him.

"You know what we need?" he asks. "We need a <u>battle plan</u>!"

BATTLE PLAN? – Yes, Because This is War!

You want to give your special needs child and your whole family – including yourself! – the best life that you can.

But there is an enemy waiting to stop you; an enemy that can take away your mental and physical health, your time and money, your relationships, your career, and all the joy in your life ... **IF** you let it.

> *You have to fight back. If you don't, you're the one who loses in the end. But if you do keep going and fight back, you win.*
> – Author and musician Alexandra Monir

The name of your enemy is **autism**. It's time to declare war against it and learn how to fight back.

Raising your child is one of the most important things you will ever do in your life. Unless you are curing cancer or bringing about world peace, you will never do anything more worthwhile, vital and demanding.

Why should you let autism stop you from meeting that challenge with all your might?

Giving your child the best life possible is one of the most loving and selfless acts you will ever perform.

Do you want autism to prevent you from achieving that goal?

Allowing yourself to have a fulfilling and satisfying life, while raising your son or daughter, is one of the greatest gifts you can give your family.

Will you allow autism to take that away from you?

This section of the book will empower you and build the battle plan you need to fight back ... and win!

Meet The Enemy

Autism is a powerful adversary. It never gets tired or distracted, or runs out of patience or money. And, as I said before, it has the power to destroy everything that you hold near and dear.

You need to understand a couple of things about your enemy.

The first is that autism doesn't care. There is no mind or force behind the disorder that you can appeal to or argue with.

Autism doesn't care that it is being unfair to you and your child. It doesn't care how nice you are, how innocent your child is, how much you love your spouse or how important your career is.

> *You may have to fight a battle more than once to win it.* – British Prime Minister Margaret Thatcher

Second, know that autism fights dirty. There are no rules and no holds barred.

Autism will use your kids against you. It will go after your weak points, try to break up your family, and kick you when you're down.

But autism is <u>not</u> invincible. You <u>can</u> successfully fight against its effects on your life. You can <u>win</u> the battles that allow you to reclaim control and build the life you want.

Victory over autism does not mean ending the disorder – it means ending the control it has had over you and your family. Victory means <u>peace</u>; peace of mind with less stress and more joy.

Don't Be A Casualty

War is serious business, even a non-military war like the one we're talking about here. People get hurt in wars. Lives can be destroyed.

And believe me, I should know; I came "this close" to losing it all. I was very nearly a casualty of autism's attacks.

When I look back at my son's early life and all the wasted, unproductive and frustrating years I spent dealing with autism, I am horrified. Back then, I let autism defeat and define me.

As I said earlier, it has taken me 18 years as a parent, and years helping countless other parents, to know what I know now.

I hope you learn from my experience and don't wait years to become a soldier in this war. You have to gear up <u>now</u>, put your battle suit on and take this war deadly seriously.

> *The true soldier fights not because he hates what is in front of him, but because he loves what is behind him.*
> – British journalist, writer & philosopher G.K. Chesterton

You are fighting <u>against</u> autism and <u>for</u> your child – the stakes couldn't be higher. This is your one shot at living the best life you can.

We live in a world where nothing is guaranteed. Anything can change in an instant. A perfectly healthy person can get run over by a truck. A successful executive can become unemployed when a company goes bankrupt.

And a parent like you can hear those four little words that turned your life upside down and inside out:

YOUR CHILD HAS AUTISM

Too many people who have heard those four words end up as casualties.

Just think of all the broken human spirits, broken marriages, broken families, lost homes and jobs, people turning to alcohol or drugs to numb the pain ... the list goes on and on. And it is all because of autism.

> *The greatest danger appears at the moment of victory. Never drop your guard.* – French emperor Napoleon Bonaparte

Well, I am <u>not</u> going to let you be autism's next casualty. You're going to <u>fight</u> and you're going to fight <u>hard</u> and smart to win.

And just like a military campaign, your victory will depend on sound preparation, a good battle plan and fearless execution.

Defeat is simply not an option.

It's like British Prime Minister Winston Churchill said when it looked like the Nazis were going to invade England – he promised to fight the invaders on the beaches, on the streets and in the hills, adding "We shall never surrender!"

So, this final section of the book is all about creating the winning battle plan that will allow you to achieve two key objectives:

1. To **successfully raise your child** and act as champion for his or her needs for as long as needed, and

2. To achieve that while building a **good life for yourself and the rest of your family.**

You may not be able to change the circumstance that put you into this war, but you <u>can</u> change the way you deal with those circumstances.

And I should note that this advice is for every parent in our situation, whether you have already achieved Acceptance and want to stay there, or are still on the path up Autism Mountain and want help to reach the top.

> *Step follows step,*
> *Hope follows Courage,*
> *Set your face towards danger,*
> *Set your heart on victory.*
> – Children's author Gail Carson Levine

The Autism War Room

Now, let's design your **Autism Battle Plan.**

First, you need to develop a "war room" mentality, where you can:

• **Analyze your strengths and advantage points,**

• **Evaluate your opponent's plan of attack, and**

• **Create your defense strategy.**

There's an old saying – "The best defense is a good offense". And **you** are the most effective and destructive weapon against autism. Just like the mother bear, there's nothing you won't do to protect your child. And you're not going to allow anything to prevent your child from having the best possible life.

> *Some people grumble that roses have thorns; I am grateful that thorns have roses.*
> – French journalist Alphonse Karr

There will be many components in your plan, all designed to help you defeat autism and reclaim your life. And you are the general in charge of putting that plan into action.

The first component of the battle plan is developing your mental preparedness.

START WITH YOURSELF – Shift Your Mindset and <u>KNOW</u> You Can Win

Earlier in this book, we talked about not allowing autism to **define or defeat** you.

Changing your perspective on autism is **the most important step** you can take in the battle against it. Knowing what you're up against and how to deal with it will keep you sane and strong. It's also essential for your success as a parent and your child's champion.

Stop and think for a moment about autism and the role it plays in your life. Does it feel like autism controls you? Do you feel like all your life decisions are based upon all the demands autism puts on you?

It doesn't have to be this way.

You can alter your viewpoint completely; from one in which autism controls <u>you</u> to another in which <u>you</u> control the impact autism has on your life. By varying your perception, you will reduce the power and influence autism has over you and the way you live your life.

No More Blame Game

Now before we get too far, don't blame yourself for allowing autism to take over your life. Remember, you were hit by that truck out of the blue and totally unprepared for the impact. It's not as if you are weak or helpless, or that you wanted this to happen – you were forced.

Autism <u>forced</u> you to change most aspects of your life to accommodate the disability and your child's needs. No one <u>would choose</u> to bring unwelcome and undesired changes into their life. Nobody <u>wants</u> to add more jobs or extra hours to an already demanding work schedule or cut back on pleasure activities like hobbies or vacations.

Tough choices were <u>imposed</u> on you. And before you knew it, your life started revolving all around autism, with no end in sight.

> *I think happiness is what makes you pretty. Period. Happy people are beautiful. They become like a mirror and they reflect that happiness.*
> – Actress Drew Barrymore

You probably felt you didn't have a choice in the matter because, in the end, there was your child and his or her needs to consider. And that had to be the top priority, above everything else.

Well, the time has come to get off the autism merry-go-round and stop it for good.

Step 1: Realize that autism doesn't own you, unless you allow it to. It's still <u>your</u> life.

Step 2: Focus on how you can **integrate** autism into your life, instead of trying to live your life around autism.

The key is to remember that you were an <u>individual</u> with wants and needs, and hopes and dreams, before having your child and you **should continue** to be an individual while raising your child.

Parenting shouldn't stop your life, even if you are parenting a child with special needs. And even though the parenting demands are tougher on us, we shouldn't be penalized for it.

You deserve a good life, as good as any other parent. You are allowed to live your life in a way that makes you happy and fulfilled.

But don't think I am telling you to "abandon" your child while you live your life. No, it's quite the opposite.

You will still be 100% committed to your child. You will continue to seek the best medical treatment, therapy and whatever else is necessary to help your child. And, surprisingly, once you change your perspective on autism and start living your life, you'll have more energy and drive to help your child.

> *Be yourself; everyone else is already taken.*
> – Poet & playwright Oscar Wilde

But what you won't do is lose <u>yourself</u> in the process. And that's what happens too often; we get wrapped up in the all-consuming world of autism, which sucks all the life and energy out of us. We end up with nothing left to give – not to ourselves, not to our kids, not to our partners.

So, it's time to stop <u>losing</u> yourself and start <u>finding</u> yourself; commit to **start living again**.

LET THE BATTLE BEGIN

During the remaining part of this section, we will examine various aspects of your life, including your relationships with your:

- **partner,**
- **child and other children, if you have any,**
- **family and friends,**
- **child's medical team, and**
- **child's teaching staff.**

In each case, we will be looking at ways you can effectively and successfully fight back against the attacks autism may throw at you.

Let's begin with **autism's personal attack on you ...**

AUTISM ATTACK PLAN #1

Autism's Objective:

- **Create constant mental turmoil and emotional upheavals in your life**

Autism's Tactics:

- **Throw multiple nuclear side effects at you while you skid and slide between the stages of denial and Acceptance**

YOUR DEFENSE STRATEGY:

Acknowledge Your Feelings

You didn't plan to have a child with autism or special needs. Nobody does.

You may feel sad, depressed, lonely or angry during periods of your life. There may be times when you secretly wish your child didn't have autism and could be like every other "normal" kid you know.

The first thing to remember is that these thoughts and feelings are perfectly normal and it's okay to have them every now and then. This does not make you a bad person or a bad parent – it just means you're human.

> *The appearance of things changes according to the emotions; and thus we see magic and beauty in them, while the magic and beauty are really in ourselves. – Poet Khalil Gibran*

Loving your child and doing your best for him/her makes you a good parent, whether your child has autism or not. Continuing to do your best in difficult circumstances makes you both a good parent and a good person.

If you find that you are constantly plagued by negative thoughts, you may find it helpful to express your feelings. There are a variety of ways to do that, such as writing in a journal or talking to a good friend or a trained, professional autism coach.

Strive for Total Acceptance

We've talked a lot about reaching the top of Autism Mountain and the wonderful place called Acceptance. To jog your memory, here's what we said way back in Section One:

Acceptance isn't about "being happy" – you will still hate the situation. The world won't be perfect, and you and your family will still be who you are. Autism won't magically stop being a problem, but you will be able to accept, adapt and thrive.

Acceptance means being realistic about today, being ready for tomorrow, and being hopeful about the future. It means believing in yourself and your family, knowing that you can handle whatever life throws at you.

Above all, Acceptance means:

- **You can look at your child and see a <u>person</u>, not a disability**

- **You can truly <u>love</u> a child who may never be "normal"**

- **You can <u>embrace</u> a life that you didn't dream about or plan for**

- **You can move on, <u>reclaim your life</u> and build a better future**

Now, I want to introduce one final thought about Acceptance that will help you get up those last few steps of the mountain and stay there.

Real Acceptance is more than accepting the fact that your child has autism.

It also encompasses <u>personal</u> acceptance; it's about coming to terms with the "new" and, most likely, stronger and determined person that you will become as you integrate autism in your life.

I don't mean that you will drastically change your personality and become someone you don't recognize. Rather, because of your experience and/or journey with autism, you will change and grow. No one stays the same. All good parents are changed by the experience of parenting.

> *Don't "dare to be different", dare to be yourself. If that doesn't make you different, then something is wrong.*
> – Writer and coach Laura Baker

But you will have <u>control</u> over how those changes occur. When you reach Acceptance, you're now in a position to make conscious, smart decisions that can positively affect your life and that of your family.

Autism isn't being imposed on you any longer. In fact, it's just the opposite; you are imposing yourself on autism.

Above all, total Acceptance means that you can look at yourself and see "you" again, not just a parent of a child with a disability.

You may even uncover new revelations about yourself, and find strengths, skills and talents you never knew existed or were possible for you. Many parents develop inner strength, more compassion towards others, an appreciation for life's simple pleasures or a renewed sense of purpose.

As I said before, no one <u>chooses</u> self-improvement through autism. But becoming a stronger, wiser and more remarkable person may be worth it.

And remember those annoying nuclear side effects? Well, they begin to lose their potency to affect you. They eventually get replaced by **"Atomic Benefits",** which are positive thoughts and emotions such as hope, optimism, joy and pride.

AUTISM ATTACK PLAN #2

Autism's Objective:

- **Stop you from having a good life**

Autism's Tactics:

- **Generate feelings of unworthiness**

- **Create an "identity" crisis for you**

- **Deny you personal fulfillment and happiness**

YOUR DEFENSE STRATEGY:

Make Yourself A Priority

This may be one of the hardest things you'll have to do, because you feel like your child should be the priority. But you <u>have</u> to do it, not for yourself but, in fact, for your child!

You need to take care of yourself, both emotionally and physically. That means trying to get at least six hours of sleep a night, eating properly and getting some exercise in.

> *Just like your body and lifestyle can be healthy or unhealthy, the same is true with your beliefs. Your beliefs can be your medicine or your poison.*
> – Speaker and behavioral scientist Dr. Steve Mariboli

You don't have to join an expensive diet plan or pay for a gym membership to do this. There is plenty of free information on healthy eating on the Internet, and one of the most beneficial and cost-efficient forms of exercise is simple walking.

A 30-minute walk, three times a week, is not only excellent for your heart; regular fresh air and exercise also benefits your mental health. You may also want to explore meditation or other relaxation techniques that will help you keep your emotional balance.

Good health is key to your emotional and physical well-being, as well as the "health" of your whole family.

Remember Who You Are

It's very easy to allow an all-encompassing challenge like autism to define you and the rest of your life. It can happen without you even realizing it.

Suddenly, you are no longer "lover of country music and great pastry chef", or "sales agent and talented handyman"... now, you are just the parent of "that kid with autism". It's important to remember that the

> *The good life doesn't come knocking on your door. Finding joy is a job.*
> – Novelist and journalist Lionel Shriver

person underneath that label is still **you**.

Like any parent, much of your life is going to be centered on your child or children from now on, but that doesn't change your past. You still sold that software, sang along with Tim McGraw, built that deck and made all of those cookies. Those things are real and permanent.

Today, you may have given up your job and have a lot less time to spend listening to the radio or organizing your tools in the garage, but you're still the same person inside. If anything, you are an even stronger and better person for having stepped up to the challenges of life with an autistic child.

Nobody can turn back time and no responsible parent can live as they did before children came along. Being the parent of an autistic child is just a new part of **you**.

Give Yourself Permission To Enjoy Life Again

Should you be happy, going shopping with friends or fishing with your buddies, with an autistic child waiting for you at home? Yes!

Some people seem to think that having a child with autism means you must be always stressed and depressed. It's bad enough when other people try to impose that thinking on you, but it's even worse when you do it to yourself.

> *One day your life will flash before your eyes. Make sure it's worth watching.*
> – Musician & graphic novelist Gerard Way

Parents of autistic children may find themselves feeling guilty for having a good time, even if it's only once in a while. But there is no reason to feel guilty; a bit of enjoyment is good for you and, believe it or not, good for your child!

Whether or not there is autism in a family, parents who take care of themselves <u>and give themselves an occasional break</u> are better able to take care of their children.

More than most parents, you need to exercise that self-care. Meeting the challenges of raising a special needs child, you can use all the strength you can get.

So, make sure you've got child care arrangements that you have confidence in, then go to that dinner with friends or birthday party for your favorite cousin. Continue to participate in hobbies, events and activities that you enjoy. It will do wonders for your emotional outlook to unload the weight of the autism burden for a few hours.

And if you continue to feel guilty, look for ways to involve your child and other family members. By giving yourself permission for joy, you will bring home new and positive energy for your whole family.

Reward Yourself

Do something nice for yourself each week, no matter how small. It could be as simple as setting aside 30 minutes to read your favorite magazine, watch your favorite comedy show or exchange e-mails with a friend.

We all need a little something to look forward to and let's face it; people in our situation work very hard taking care of our families, and <u>we are worthy</u> of a little treat every week!

Again, it comes down to having a healthy respect for yourself and the circumstances you are handling, day after day. Give yourself the credit, and the reward, that you deserve.

YOU AND YOUR PARTNER – Co-Supporters & Team Leaders

Maintaining a healthy and fulfilling marriage or relationship while raising a child with special needs is no easy task. Every relationship needs to be nurtured and cared for but, with the time-consuming and constant demands of having child with autism, it often seems impossible.

This can create a weak point where the pressures of autism's attacks can turn a small crack into a deep divide.

But a solid relationship is worth fighting for. It can be the foundation of a strong family and a key to helping each family member, including your special needs child, have the best life possible.

This is your partner in a challenging, life-long task. And more importantly, **your partner is the only person who knows exactly what you're going through and loves your child as much as you do.**

> *I'm willing to die for the woman I love. I just want to take 75 years to do it. – Comic writer Jarod Kintz*

Remember, you were a couple before becoming a family. While your lives change when you become parents, you're still in a relationship together. **If autism tries to take that away from you, you've got to fight back!**

AUTISM ATTACK PLAN #3

Autism's Objective:
- **Create constant mental turmoil and emotional upheavals in your marriage**

Autism's Tactics:
- **Break the foundation of your marriage**

- **Destroy the love you have for each other**

- **Create enough friction and tension to turn you against each other**

YOUR DEFENSE STRATEGY:

Make Your Relationship a Priority

Don't allow the disability to become the focus for your relationship. You and your partner got together because you love each other, not because you have a job to do. Remember what your relationship is really based on. It's important to stay connected to each other.

A strong marriage or relationship is your best defense against autism. If you can keep it from becoming "child-centered" or "disability-centered", you'll be even better parents for it.

You need to take care of each other. This is a partnership, so you both need to eat right, sleep well, be honest and have patience and affection for each other.

Some actions, like changing your eating habits or taking up a new hobby, like bowling, are easier and more effective when you do them together. It's another way to support one another and it will give you common ground and more time together.

Every Marriage Gets Tested

Remember, sharing your life with another person isn't always easy. No marriage or relationship is perfect. All will be tested at some point by something; it could be unemployment, infidelity, illness, or one of a thousand other problems.

Autism is your test. Make sure your relationship passes it.

A major challenge like autism has the ability to either make you stronger as a couple or tear you apart. Keep in mind; it will test you individually as well as both of you as a couple.

> *You're not obligated to win. You're obligated to keep trying. To do the best you can do every day.*
> – Singer-songwriter Jason Mraz

A good relationship is worth the effort to keep it healthy. You're stronger together than apart.

Communication Is Key

It's really important to actually <u>talk</u> to each other and not just have a polite conversation. There is a big difference between the two!

> *Trust is the glue of life. It's the most essential ingredient in effective communication. It's the foundational principle that holds all relationships.*
> – Management guru Steve Covey

There is also a world of difference between being honest and being hurtful, and between anger and disrespect. As much as you can when emotions are strong, try to give your partner the same respect and consideration that <u>you</u> want to have from him or her.

Even at the risk of hurt feelings, though, it is important to trust each other enough to speak the truth.

Let your partner know how you are <u>really</u> feeling and when the stress of autism and its side-effects is really getting to you.

Don't expect the other person to read your mind or figure out your mood from clues that you drop – you both have better ways to spend your time and energy.

Give Each Other Permission to Be Human

The responsibilities of raising a child with autism can create a lot of stress for you and your partner as individuals as well as for your relationship. Give each other permission to "blow off steam" and vent that stress now and again.

> We all take different paths in life, but no matter where we go, we take a little of each other everywhere.
> – Country singer Tim McGraw

It's important to get those negative feelings on the table. But don't judge each other or take it personally in the heat of the moment.

Give each other breaks and "time outs" when one is having a bad day or feeling overwhelmed. Take over a task for your partner if you can, and lighten the load for a few hours or even a couple of days.

Schedule Some Couple Time

> A fine glass vase goes from treasure to trash the moment it is broken. Fortunately, something else happens to you and me. Pick up your pieces. Then, help me gather mine.
> – Armenian writer Vera Nazarian

Wish you had more time together as a couple? Then take it, without guilt. Every couple needs some time together without outside pressures to re-connect and keep the emotional and communication bonds strong.

Go on a date with each other. It doesn't have to be fancy or expensive; a movie or a meal at a local diner or restaurant is fine. And an old-fashioned picnic in the park with some sandwiches and chips can be very romantic.

If possible, schedule "date nights" for yourselves on a weekly or monthly basis. Write it on the calendar. Hire a child caregiver for a few hours or ask a friend or family member to stay with your child.

Or, if you have an older son/daughter who is dependable and mature enough, ask them. Do something nice for him/her in return. In fact, you can make this a "part time" job for him/her and pay a nominal salary. It would give your older children some extra pocket money for things they want to do or buy and allow you to have a getaway with your partner. It's a win/win for the entire family.

Above all, when you are on your date, do <u>not</u> discuss your child and/or children. Have a conversation about the two of you, without bringing up the kids. It will probably be the first time you've done that in years.

Participate in activities that you enjoy. Do some of the things you did when you were dating. Take a walk together. Have fun again. Feel good about each other.

> Funny how we take it for granted that we know all there is to know about another person, just because we see them frequently or because of some strong emotional tie.
> – Screenwriter Robert Bloch

Appreciate and Be Affectionate With Each Other

Show each other appreciation for all the wonderful or demanding things you are doing as partners and parents. Tell each other "You're doing a great job" every once in a while. Thank each other for acts of kindness, such as "Thanks for letting me sleep late this morning. I really appreciate it". It's always nice to hear compliments, especially from your spouse.

Be affectionate with each other; a kiss in the morning or evening, an affectionate touch on the cheek as you pass each other in the hall – these little gestures can go a long way.

E-mail or text each other now and again to show that you're thinking about your partner in a loving way.

Seek Outside Help If You Need To

Sometimes it helps to get some outside support. It may benefit the both of you to speak to a professional to get some new perspective and insights.

This is not an admission of failure and it does not mean your relationship is in trouble. It only signifies that you care about each other enough to work on your problems, and that you are mature enough to know when you need a hand.

Relationship Maintenance

Now, all of the strategies above apply to any kind of relationship, but there are certain extra steps you can take if you are partners in a strong marriage or relationship where you truly share the burdens and responsibilities together.

> Compromise, if not the spice of life, is its solidity. It is what makes nations great and marriages happy.
> – Poet Phyllis McGinley

If you're fortunate enough to be in this situation, take advantage of the tremendous benefits it offers, and don't let it slip through your fingers for want of a little extra effort:

Build A Solid Team

If you and your partner are rock-solid, you are not only partners, but co-captains of your child's team. Together, you need to decide the best ways to handle all of the issues that autism has raised in your lives, how to integrate it into your family's life, and how you want to raise your child.

You both need to be on the same page. Remember, you're on the same team and leading that team. Even when you disagree, autism is your enemy, not each other.

Keep An Open Mind

Accept the fact that you may have different approaches, perspectives and points of view. You both want the best for your child, so accept your differences, build on your strengths and share your common points of view. You <u>will</u> have to compromise at times. So will your partner.

Develop A Team Strategy

Create a core strategy or game plan and implement it. This will be a "living" plan that will change as your child grows up and the challenges and/or issues change. What was once certain may become questionable ... new questions will come up ... your lives will not stay the same. So, follow your game plan now, but be prepared to keep updating it as time goes on.

You're In It Together

As partners and teammates, you both have to take shared responsibility for your child. No parent should have 100% responsibility; both parents should be involved in the child's life. They should share accountability for important things like attending IEP meetings, medical visits, etc.

> *My success has been based, from the very beginning, on partnerships.*
> – Microsoft founder Bill Gates

No parent is allowed to "opt out" of their obligations just because the other parent is "doing such a great job" of managing everything. You have to be fair and respectful of each other, and step up to your share of the duties, or resentment and anger will set in.

Create Fair and Equitable Responsibilities

You have to assume those tasks that work for the both of you and are <u>fair</u>. It may be helpful to actually write down who will be responsible for managing different aspects of your child's daily routine as well as household chores.

For example, if mom is home taking care of the child and other household tasks during the day, then dad should help out in the evening. Even if dad works long hours, he can do something small like wash the dishes or read the autistic child a bedtime story and put him/her to bed.

Also, if you have other children, have them help out as well. They can assist you with household duties and you can pay them an allowance for their contribution.

Every member of the family should be a member of the team and should help out accordingly, helping take care of your autistic child and contributing to your joint, team successes.

Everything Is Negotiable

With so much to do, some things are going to fall through the cracks. That's how life is. What you and your partner have to decide is which failures are <u>not</u> acceptable; which of them are "deal breakers".

Decide what you can live with and what you can't allow. Maybe the carpet does not have to be vacuumed every day, but the dogs <u>must</u> be taken for a walk.

Discuss the differences between what you need and what you want. Your family <u>needs</u> to eat dinner every day and you <u>want</u> them to have hot, home-cooked meals. So, you'll have dinner daily, and most of the time you'll cook it

> *We should never negotiate out of fear, but we should never fear to negotiate.*
> – President John F. Kennedy

yourselves. However, you agree that you'll go out for dinner on Friday nights, order in pizza every Tuesday and pop a frozen dinner in the microwave or toaster oven every once in a while.

Agree on the important things for both of you. One of you may care more about getting the laundry done before the weekend. The other would rather use the time for preparing food ahead of time. This is where compromise is so important; you both have to make sacrifices for the good of the marriage and the family. No one should feel like they got the "raw end" of the deal.

Put everything on the table and understand that it's all negotiable and all subject to change. In fact, your responsibilities will definitely alter over time, as your child's needs transform.

As with anything to do with relationships, every couple and every situation is unique. Do what's best for you, your marriage and family.

YOU AND YOUR AUTISTIC CHILD – The Battle of the Bond

Of all of the terrible things autism can do to you, undermining the love between you and your special needs child is the worst, most heartless and devastating attack of all.

> *There are only two lasting bequests we can hope to give our children. One of these is roots; the other, wings.*
> – Journalist Hodding Carter

As we've said throughout this book, a child with autism <u>needs</u> your love, support and strength, and <u>you</u> need to have a loving, warm relationship with your child.

When the attacks staged by autism are allowed to break that bond, everyone suffers. There are no winners, only losers.

So, if you're going to fight and win on only one front – <u>this is it</u>!

Again, the most important thing you can do as a parent is to **separate the diagnosis from the child**, the disability from the person.

If you look only at the behavior and challenges, you are allowing autism to be the focus of your relationship. The positive alternative is accepting your child for who he or she is, understanding they cannot be blamed for their disability, and taking autism as another aspect of your lives together.

When you can do that, you're halfway to beating autism for good!

AUTISM ATTACK PLAN #4

Autism's Objective:

- **Break the bond between you and your child**

Autism's Tactics:

- **Overwhelm and frustrate you with the demands of raising a special needs child**

- **Replace love with negative emotions such as frustration and anger**

- **Make you see the "disability" and not your child**

YOUR DEFENSE STRATEGY:

Love Your Child

First and foremost, last and always – loving your child is your purpose in life as a parent. Never let autism stop you from seeing the person behind the disability and loving him or her unconditionally.

In your mind, stand up and punch autism in the nose! Tell it you will never let it break your bond, that your child is a worthwhile, loved and wonderful human being, and that autism will never be allowed to define either of you.

Accept children the way we accept trees – with gratitude, because they are a blessing, but not with expectations or desires. You don't expect trees to change; you love them as they are.
– Chilean-American novelist Isabel Allende

Be Extra Patient With Your Child

Second, you have to always keep in mind that your child has a neurological disorder that affects normal brain function. This condition can affect your child's cognitive, communication and social skills as well as physical abilities.

This is **NOT** your child's fault. He or she did not <u>choose</u> autism, any more than you did. **AUTISM** is the problem, <u>not</u> your child.

It is a disorder that may limit your child's ability to process information correctly, understand his/her surroundings and to learn new things. He or she may have a very short attention span and not pay attention to details or surrounding people. Children who are non-verbal may find it difficult to express their needs and wants to you.

No two children are alike on the spectrum. You will have to get to know your child's behavior, likes and dislikes, and routines. This is when your detective skills we discussed earlier can be very helpful.

When it comes to learning, your child may not progress as much or as fast as you wish. It may be necessary to repeat the same task several times, even over many days or weeks, to allow your child to understand what you are asking of him/her. You may have to break down a simple task to its smallest components in order for your child to learn the skill. It may take weeks or months to see results from all your efforts.

Anyone who does anything to help a child in his life is a hero to me.
– Children's TV host Fred Rogers

At times, you may be frustrated, angry or annoyed by your child's behavior or inability to learn and adapt to new things. It may be helpful to take a deep breath or walk away if you need to for a little while. It's better to "blow off a little steam" in another room, than in front of your child.

Again, your child is not deliberately trying to anger or upset you. Your child is <u>not</u> an autistic disorder, but a person. The disorder is a <u>barrier</u> between you and your son or daughter; and it's not an easy barrier to overcome.

Don't Treat Your Child As A Science Experiment

Part of separating your child from the disability is realizing that his or her life is more than just a series of treatment plans.

Just like any other child, yours deserves to be a

To be in your children's memories tomorrow, you must be in their lives today.
– 'Minister of Joy' Barbara Johnson

kid – to have some fun, enjoy the experiences of life and just relax sometimes. And, you know what? You deserve that, too.

You don't have to spend every waking moment analyzing your child's behavior or trying to modify it. They get enough of that in school with constant observation and therapy. Just like you, your child needs a little downtime now and again.

So, have some fun! Play with each other. Take a break from all the therapy and do something silly. Throw pillows at each other while lying on the bed. Do some arts and crafts or finger painting. Blow bubbles and pop them.

Remember, not every activity has to have a purpose or accomplish a goal. Fun is a lifelong learning process, and an important part of every child's life.

Bottom line: stick out your tongue at autism and **have a good time with your kid**!

Focus on the Quality of Your Child's Life

I've mentioned several times the idea of giving your child the best life he/she can have. Part of that, obviously, is seeking out the best medical treatments, education and therapy you can find for them. Another part is building in the fun and joy of life we talked about.

There is something else you can do as parents that will help create a better future for your child – help her or him to develop the daily living skills that will allow them to become more independent and self-sufficient.

> *The purpose of life is to live it, to taste experience to the utmost, to reach out eagerly and without fear for newer and richer experience.*
> – First Lady Eleanor Roosevelt

That's not just teaching them how to care for themselves as much as possible, but also how to interact with the public and function in the "real" world. Take your child with you into the community and expose him/her to everyday living situations such as going to the supermarket or department store, taking the bus, and crossing the street safely.

Every experience, no matter how ordinary, can create new learning opportunities. Sometimes, we forget how easily things come to us and take it for granted our children will learn as effortlessly as we did. Parents need to start looking at things from their child's perspective, in order to help him/her develop essential skills and abilities.

If your child can travel, take him or her with you as much as possible. If you can't go on an extended vacation, how about a day trip to the zoo, to the movies or an amusement park?

Some movie theatres now offer special shows and show times for families with special needs children and adults. During the movie, the lights may be on, the sound turned down and audience members are invited to get up and dance, walk, shout and sing. In this comfortable and stress-free environment, you don't have worry to about upsetting other movie goers and can actually sit back and enjoy the show.

And some amusement parks provide special passes for individuals with special needs which allow them to go the front of the line at rides. This is so beneficial because your child won't have to stand or sit in lines for extended periods of times and experience muscle fatigue, frustration or a possible meltdown. How great is that?

Focus on the "Here and Now"

It's easy for any parent to get hung up on the future. Some put enormous amounts of effort into getting their kids into the right pre-school that will lead to the best public school, the best high school and set them up for Harvard University – all when they're three years old!

For parents in our situation, the challenge is a little different. We tend to look to the future with uncertainty, concerned about what will happen to our children in the long term, and convinced that their lives are going to be limited.

The truth is that nobody knows what the future will hold for your child, for my child, or for anyone else's. The only thing we can say for sure is this … if we give up on our kids, we are reducing their chances of living their happiest, most successful life.

> I sometimes wake in the early morning and listen to the soft breathing of my child, and I think to myself, this is one thing I will never regret. I carry that quiet with me all day long.
> – Artist Brian Andreas

Like every other parent, we have to invest in the unknown. All children have potential and we can't say where it might take them. All we can do is love and try to give them the most skills and confidence we can, to help them make the most of whatever lies ahead.

Autism might, in fact, limit your child's future. That's no reason for you to limit it as well. Just as everyone should plan ahead for their retirement while they are still young and working, so should parents lay the foundations and develop plans for a safe and secure tomorrow for their children.

The trick is not to obsess about it, or let tomorrow's concerns rob you of today's joys.

Focus on the here and now – doing the best for your child in the current circumstances, while maintaining your hope for a positive future.

Celebrate Your Child's Uniqueness

No two children are alike. Each one is special and has unique qualities.

Look at it that way and you'll realize your special needs child is just like every other kid on the planet – needing love, respect and understanding, and deserving to be celebrated for just who he or she is.

I'm not saying you should celebrate autism. Remember, you're celebrating your <u>child</u> and your child is separate from the <u>disability</u>, right?

So, instead of focusing on what your child can **not** do, think about what they **can** do. Look for the special qualities and the little things that bring them comfort or happiness.

It's not just their "needs" that make our children special. Find what is wonderful and unique about your child and celebrate it!

YOU AND YOUR OTHER CHILDREN – Autism's Sneak Attack

Your other children are special, too.

It has been said that every child has "special" needs. Whether or not they have a disability, all children need and deserve the love and support of their parents, and to know they hold a special place in your hearts.

However, the demands of living with autism can steal away the time and energy you would otherwise have for the rest of your kids. Siblings often feel neglected or unappreciated because parents tend to spend most of their time managing the needs of their autistic child.

> *How can there be too many children? That's like saying there are too many flowers.*
> – Poverty activist Mother Teresa

That's autism's great "sneak attack" on your family – coming up under the walls and trying to weaken your team from within.

Knowing that attack is coming (and it hits virtually every family dealing with autism) allows you to be on your guard and stop this underhanded assault as soon as it begins.

AUTISM ATTACK PLAN #5

Autism's Objective:

- **Destroy your family unit**

Autism's Tactics:

- **Create jealousy and resentment among siblings**

- **Undermine your relationships with your other children**

YOUR DEFENSE STRATEGY:

Use the Power of Parental Love

Children who are confident that they have your unconditional love are a lot less likely to feel jealousy or resentment. You should demonstrate your love by being affectionate with your other children. Hugs and kisses as well as high fives and pats on the back are great for everyone.

Encourage and develop the skills, talents and abilities of your other children. Show a sincere interest in what they're doing, whether it's a new sport, hobby or part time job they've just started. Ask about their days and "how things are going". Make sure they're performing well in school and keeping up with their studies. Know who their friends are and where they do their socializing. It all comes down to showing your other children that you care as much about them as you do your autistic child.

Praise and recognition are also wonderful. You should thank them for getting good grades, helping you with some household tasks or taking care of their sibling when you are away. Do something special as a token of your appreciation, and talk about them as the "best kids", "great helpers" and "so mature and responsible", particularly in front of other people.

Take the Time Whenever Possible

You should set aside time to spend with your other children on a regular basis. It can be as simple as watching a movie on cable or a DVD together at home or going for a burger at their favorite fast food restaurant.

> *The ultimate test of a moral society is the kind of world that it leaves to its children.* – German theologian and Nazi fighter Dietrich Bonhoeffer

You can participate in an activity or event that your other children enjoy. Pick something they like but often don't get the opportunity to do because your autistic child isn't able to take part.

If possible, schedule these activities ahead of time and mark them on the same calendar you use for your autistic child's therapy appointments, etc. This makes it the <u>family</u> calendar and shows your other children that what you do with them is just as important as what you do with your autistic child.

Take photos or videos with your cell phone so everybody can remember these fun and happy times. Put one of these photos up on the fridge or make it your computer's screen saver.

Talk and LISTEN

Your best defense against autism's sneak attack on your family is keeping the lines of communication open.

Talk to your other children openly about how they are dealing with the autism or feel about having an autistic sibling. Just like you don't want to be judged for your occasional weakness or negativity, don't judge your children for their natural feelings. They need to know that you are not only <u>talking</u> to them, but <u>listening</u> to what they have to say.

While many parents have a natural instinct to protect their other children from the stresses and challenges of raising a special needs child, you should know that your other kids are seeing, hearing and thinking about <u>everything</u> that happens in your home. They can feel when you're upset, stressed or frustrated, which can make them worried about the future of their family.

So, be as honest as possible with your children, depending on their ages. When you explain and share your feelings, you help them understand how to handle their own experiences and you open the door to two-way communications.

Watch for the Signs

When children feel frustrated, jealous or ignored, they may act out in many ways. Some may take their feelings out on the autistic child, refusing to communicate or spend time with him or her. Others may get involved with a bad group at school, start using drugs or alcohol, or get failing grades.

> *Children are our most valuable natural resource.*
> – President Herbert Hoover

All of these actions are cries for attention. It may be the only way they know how to get their parents' attention.

Just as adults can be good people in a bad situation, so can children. But they don't always have the maturity and emotional strength to handle those situations well.

It doesn't mean they are "bad kids", just that they are having a tough time. If you're having difficulty getting them through it, don't hesitate to seek appropriate professional help.

Help Build Bonds

It's also important for parents to encourage a good relationship between the siblings and the autistic child. Look for fun activities and events that all your children can enjoy together. It's important that they spend quality time with each other and develop their own special bond.

Siblings can be great teachers and homework helpers. They can present things in much more creative and interesting ways than most parents can. And they possess two key traits that most parents lack: youth and energy. Enough said!

But don't be upset if they have their ups and downs. Siblings in most families, with or without autism involved, don't always get along as they grow up together. Their interactions will change as they grow up, so it's important to let the relationships develop on their own, natural terms.

> *Having children is like living in a frat house - nobody sleeps, everything's broken, and there's a lot of throwing up.*
> – Comedian Ray Romano

Like the Song Says - "Love Will Keep Us Together"

Doing things together that make your other children feel special and wanted will strengthen your family and help avoid jealousy. Allow them to be the center of attention now and then. Praise and support their efforts to be good siblings.

When you take part in typical, ordinary, family activities, you help make everyone feel like a "normal" family. Trips to the park, movies or beach. Visiting relatives and friends. Family barbeques. Having birthday parties and other family celebrations.

All these things create a feeling of togetherness and normalcy, which is what you want your family to experience. After all, that's what you are: a family.

Creating a happy and loving family for _all_ your children is the right thing to do for everyone and can have wonderful long-term benefits. You can prevent resentment and help your other children to build wonderful memories of spending quality time alone with you and other family members.

Thinking About the Future

It's not something we like to think about, but deep down inside parents of special needs children know that they will get old and, at some point, be unable to care for their disabled child. Many parents may look toward their other children to take on that responsibility when mom and dad age or pass away.

> _Our task as parents is to become the architects of the future._
> – Kenyan statesman Jomo Kenyatta

However, parents should understand that they cannot automatically assume or insist that their other children take full responsibility for their autistic child.

The siblings will have lives, careers and possibly families of their own as they get older. It may not be possible for them to manage the day-to-day responsibilities of caring for their autistic brother or sister.

What you _can_ ask for is that your other children maintain an active role and presence in their autistic sibling's life. Wherever your disabled child may be at the time, his or her siblings can help ensure that good care is being provided, and can give him or her extra love and attention.

Knowing that caring brothers and sisters are keeping an eye on your special needs child will give you priceless comfort and peace of mind. You can help ensure that future by building and strengthening your family's bonds today.

YOU AND YOUR FAMILY AND FRIENDS – Don't Let the Bonds Break

Friendships are like tea bags – you don't know how strong they are until you're in hot water! When the chips are down and times are tough, you find out who is really there for you.

The support of others around can help you make it through the hard days, aid you in making good decisions, and provide the physical and emotional breaks we all need now and then.

> *You are born into your family, and your family is born into you. No returns, no exchanges.*
> – Novelist Elizabeth Berg

But, just as it can do with your immediate family, autism can attack those relationships, break down your alliances and rob you of your allies.

If it can succeed in isolating you, autism will have made it harder for you to deal with the challenges of your life, and less likely that you and your family can have the good life you want and deserve.

Your extended family and friends are lifelines to the world around you; we can't afford to let autism cut those lines and push you into a lonely corner!

This is the autism version of "psychological warfare" – trying to use your own mind against you. A positive attitude is key to winning this battle.

AUTISM ATTACK PLAN #6

Autism's Objective:

- **Isolate you from your family and friends**

Autism's Tactics:

- **Make you feel alone and that no one can help you**

- **Create feelings of powerlessness**

YOUR DEFENSE STRATEGY:

Don't Isolate Yourself

Your friends and family don't like or love you less because you have a child with autism. In fact, they probably admire and respect you more than ever after seeing how difficult it can be to raise a child with special needs.

And the people who really love you are not offering pity, they are giving empathy – they are putting

> *Families break up when they start getting hints that you are not giving, but missing the hints that you do.*
> – Poet Robert Frost

71

themselves in your shoes, as far as they can, and trying to figure out how they can help.

Don't shut these people out of your life, and don't shut yourself in. Reach out and you will find many hands waiting to take yours.

Spending time with those who love you is good for any person, but particularly important for those in stressful and potentially isolating situations.

Above all, choose to spend time with people who make you feel at ease. If certain friends or family members make you feel uncomfortable by staring, making remarks or over-reacting to your child's behavior, don't associate with them. Maintain positive relationships with those who understand your child's condition and support your family.

When autism makes you feel cut off from the rest of the world, you're in danger of losing the important fight to reclaim your life. You need those connections; they're worth the effort.

Ask For Help When You Need It

Unless you have a secret identity and a cape in your closet, you're not a superhero. And without superpowers, no parent of an autistic child is going to make it through the rest of their lives without help.

Of course, we all have our pride and want to be able to stand on our own two feet, take care of our families and do things our way.

But there are going to be times when all the challenges and stress get on top of you, and you just need an extra pair of hands to help you though. There's no shame in asking for and accepting help.

> *I always hear people talk about 'dysfunctional families.' It annoys me, because it makes you think that somewhere there's this magical family where everyone gets along, and no one ever screams things they don't mean, and there's never a time when sharp objects should be hidden.*
> *Well, I'm sorry, but that family doesn't exist. The best you can really hope for is a family where everyone's problems, big and small, work together. Kind of like an orchestra where every instrument is out of tune, in exactly the same way, so you don't really notice.*
> – Film & TV writer Neal Shusterman

Contrary to popular belief, it's not a sign of weakness. It's actually a sign of strength and courage to share your needs with others.

So call your best friend and ask him/her to pick up some groceries for you at the supermarket when he/she's shopping for his/her family. Or ask your neighbor to meet your child's bus if you have to leave work later than usual.

And it's perfectly okay to let your mom take your child to his/her doctor's appointment if you can't get time off from work. Most physicians will be fine with having someone else with the child as long as they know in advance.

Also, when your child is in the examining room with his/her doctor, have your mom call you on your cell phone. You can speak directly to the doctor about your child's medical needs and your mom won't have to worry about saying the wrong thing.

Schedule Some "Me Time"

When family and good friends ask what they can do to help, you can do yourself a huge favor by asking for one thing -- a few hours of "me time". When was the last time you had a manicure, shot some pool with your buddies, or simply lingered over a cup of coffee without worrying that you have to rush home?

Take full advantage of these kind gestures and opportunities. Do something that you truly enjoy, or that you simply never get the opportunity to do in your busy life. You will feel better and your friend or family member will know they're doing something that really makes a difference.

The simplest way of arranging this kind of "personal break time" is usually to ask your friends and family to come and take care of, or play with, your child in your home. Familiar surroundings will make it easier for your autistic child and your wonderful caregiver.

You will know that your child is safe and well-cared for, and that you don't have to pay for child care. Does life get any better than this?

YOU AND YOUR CHILD'S EDUCATION – Don't Be Overwhelmed

Just about every parent of a child with autism ends up feeling overwhelmed by the large and complex world of special education. For parents of typical children, the path is familiar and clearly defined: pre-school, elementary school, junior high or middle school, high school and then, college.

But in our case, you never know what to expect, except that it will be more complex and frustrating. Some parents may find themselves struggling to locate the right school where their child can receive a good and appropriate education. Others may be in a constant battle to ensure their child receives the therapy and other services he/she requires.

> *Some days are just hard and you want to go asleep and wake up a week from now knowing the problem is gone. Everyone feels like that once in a while. Life can be overwhelming.*
> – Australian humorist Belle Aurora

As with any large and complicated organization, you may find bureaucratic barriers in the education system. And navigating them successfully can be a full-time job, not to mention difficult and aggravating at times.

And then, there is the task of learning about all the individuals who function in the world of special education. There are a variety of teachers, therapists and other educational and training experts whose roles and responsibilities you have to become familiar with.

Parents also have to learn new terms for teaching as it pertains to special education. What is ABA? What is sensory integration? What are gross motor skills? What is an assistive communication device? And the list goes on and on.

With so many different things, ideas and opinions coming at you, so many decisions to make for your child, and a never-ending pile of information to read and understand, it's the very exceptional person who doesn't feel like they're in over their head.

Autism can turn your frustration, confusion and sometimes anger into an assault on your emotional and physical resources. It's like a mass attack coming toward you, overwhelming your defenses and not giving you time to think clearly or react effectively.

Are you choosing the right educational path for your child? Do you know and understand enough to choose wisely? Autism gets you asking these questions until you lose your self-confidence in your ability to take the right way forward or feel like giving up.

> *Never doubt that a small group of committed people can change the world. Indeed, it's the only thing that ever has.*
> – Anthropologist Margaret Mead

However, if you learn how to handle this new world and work effectively with school administrators, teaching staff and other educational faculty, you can succeed in securing a sound and proper education that meets your child's needs.

AUTISM ATTACK PLAN #7

Autism's Objective:

- **Prevent you from developing the best educational program for your child**

Autism's Tactics:

- **Overwhelm you with the numerous responsibilities of educating your child**

- **Swamp you with learning about the different aspects of "special education"**

- **Frustrate and discourage you as advocate for your child**

YOUR DEFENSE STRATEGY:

Become an Involved Parent

Getting to know and develop good, working relationships with your child's teacher, classroom paraprofessionals and therapists is one of the smartest and most effective things you can do for yourself and your child. Most times, teachers and classroom staff spend more time with your child than you do. They observe your child in a variety of settings and time-periods during the school day.

Teachers and teaching staff can help with understanding how autism affects your child in the classroom. They can offer advice on which academic activities and lesson plans are appropriate, based on your child's cognitive ability and personality.

> *Anyone who stops learning is old, whether at twenty or eighty. Anyone who keeps learning stays young.*
> – Industrialist Henry Ford

And the teaching staff is an invaluable resource for personal knowledge – what your child likes to eat or drink at school, how he or she interacts with peers, how their social skills are developing, etc. They can serve as your on-site detective(s) at school.

You can also schedule occasional visits to school and observe your child, without him or her knowing you're there. It's very helpful to see your child in a school setting, away from home, among peers and school staff. You might be pleasantly surprised to see a whole different side of your child as he/she interacts with others.

And remember, you don't have to wait for an official IEP meeting or Parent/Teacher conference to meet with your child's teaching staff and discuss your child's education. Meeting periodically throughout the school year is fine as long as it is convenient for all of you.

Learn From The "Therapy" Team

All of your child's therapists can be equally as helpful and valuable to you, regardless of whether they specialize in speech, physical, occupational or behavioral therapy. So take advantage of their expertise, and don't be afraid to ask questions.

For many parents, this may be their first experience working with any kind of therapist. You're not expected to know everything about what therapists do and how they work on specific goals with your child.

When you speak with each therapist, tell him/her what areas you think your child needs help in. They will welcome your input. And after they've had time to evaluate your child, ask them to follow up with you and discuss their assessment to determine, together, what should be done to help your child. Also, ask them to explain the kind of exercises or activities they will be working on in school.

Therapists can also assist you in developing a customized, therapeutic program for your child that you can implement at home. It's beneficial for you to support and reinforce the skills they are trying to develop for your child in school.

- Physical therapists can suggest exercises that might help your child develop his/her gross motor skills, such as using a small trampoline at home to develop muscle strength, balance and coordination.

- Occupational therapists can give you low-cost, therapeutic exercises that can develop your child's fine motor skills. For example, have your child pour a breakfast cereal, like Cheerios, into a bowl. Then he/she should pick up a few pieces of the cereal, one at a time, using their fingers, from a placemat to add on top. This OT therapy didn't cost any money because you had the cereal in your home already. But by spending an extra 5 minutes of your time during breakfast, you helped your child tremendously.

- Speech therapists may suggest strategies to help your child communicate more effectively. This is especially true of non-verbal children – they may benefit from additional methods besides Picture Exchange Communication System (PECS), such as iPad apps.

- Behavioral therapists can give you strategies for calming your child down in the midst of a meltdown. They can help you understand what is triggering these reactions and how to avoid or reduce these triggers.

Create A Winning Partnership

All of these educators and therapists will be more helpful and involved with you when you come forward as an engaged partner. Tell and show them that you want to work with them. Be open, honest and approachable and they will be the same in return. Discuss best practices for communicating and building a successful partnership.

And it's best to form these partnerships early in the school year, while your child and teaching staff are settling in and getting to know each other. It's extremely helpful if you could provide, what I call, a "cheat sheet" on your child.

Basically, it's a short list of things about your child and his/her behavior that the teaching staff will find extremely helpful. It can be done on a piece of paper or index card, whatever works best for you, and it can be as simple as this:

Child's Name: Julie Daniels

Communication Skills: Julie is non-verbal. When she is hungry, she makes little sounds and holds her stomach.

Physical Abilities: Julie walks slowly. She likes to hold someone's hand when she walks.

Food and Meals: Julie doesn't like sandwiches and orange juice. She likes apples, chocolate milk and hamburgers. She needs assistance with eating utensils during lunch.

Behaviors: Julie doesn't like loud sounds. She covers her ears when it is too loud. If Julie gets upset, take her to the bathroom and let her play with the water in the sink basin for a few minutes. It calms her down very fast.

It may not seem like a lot of information to you, but this insight into your child and his/her behavior is priceless for the teaching staff.

You have to remember that each teacher may have anywhere from 6 to 12 students in his/ her class, while each therapist may work with as many as 50 students each school year. It's very hard for them to learn about each student's personality, likes/dislikes and behavior in a short period of time. So, anything a parent can do to help them is very much appreciated.

Set Realistic Expectations

It's very important for you and your child's teacher and therapists to set realistic goals for your child. And parents have to realize that these dedicated professionals are not miracle workers. Just as we discussed about the "Fix-it Tour", we have to manage our expectations. If your child is non-verbal, it's unrealistic to think he/she is going to start speaking or saying words in just a few weeks of working with a speech therapist.

> *The mind is not a pot to be filled, but a fire to be kindled.*
> – Ancient Greek historian Plutarch

But by working closely together as a team, everyone can give your child a chance to be the best person he/she can be. And even if progress is slow, you'll all celebrate the small achievements along the way and the efforts your child is making towards success.

Good Communication is Key

The most effective way to communicate with your child's teacher, classroom staff and/ or therapists is also one of the simplest - a notebook. You can purchase a simple spiral notebook at any department or office supply store, for probably less than a dollar. It's also good to buy a business size folder to place school bulletins or notices that may be sent home by the school's administrative staff.

The communication notebook is very easy to use. Each day, your child's teacher should write a brief note summarizing your child's activities. The notebook can also give your teacher a place to inform you about school events and activities. The daily note may be no more than 3 – 5 sentences. For example:

"Johnny had a good day. He ate all his meals and drank all his juices. He had gym and speech therapy. The parent/teacher conference is on Tuesday. Please let us know if you can attend."

Knowing what kind of a day your child had is so beneficial. Many parents would be lost without this important information, especially for parents of non-verbal children.

> *Next in importance to freedom and justice is public education, without which neither freedom nor justice can be maintained.*
> – President James Garfield

Once the teacher has done his/her part, it becomes your turn. Needless to say, most teachers work hard and don't get much spare time during the day. So if she/he took time at the end of the school day to write you a brief note, you should do the same. It's a matter of mutual respect.

Your note can also be as brief as three to five sentences. You can comment on your child's activities during the day or address any special concerns or issues you may have. You can also suggest new skills for your child to work on in school or ask for an update on IEP goals. Whatever you want to write is fine. There doesn't have to be an agenda item. Most teachers just appreciate your interest and input.

Keep in mind that most teachers have anywhere from 6 to 12 children in a class, <u>each with a different set of behaviors on the spectrum</u>. Your daily notes and feedback can help them do the best for your child.

For those of you who prefer not to write in a notebook, there may be other options. Discuss the possibility of communicating via text messages or e-mail. Some people actually find that quicker and easier than using a physical notepad.

It's also a good idea for your child's therapists to use a communication notebook as well. Some therapists may want to create one for themselves; others are fine with the teacher's notebook. The point is to have <u>regular communication</u> with your child's team members at school.

And remember, there's always the phone. Most teachers and therapists don't mind speaking with parents during their break or when they have some free time during the day.

Respect the Teaching Professionals

Last but not least, maintain a pleasant demeanor when you talk to your child's teacher, therapist or a member of the teaching or administrative staff. Be courteous, approachable and smile. This applies even if your time is short, like when you're dropping

> *One teacher, one book, one pen can change the world.*
> – Children's rights activist Malala Yousafzai

your child off at school or running late for work.

Remember, these people are not your enemy – <u>autism</u> is.

In fact, teachers and therapists can be some of your best allies. They are hard-working experts who want to help you and your child in any way possible. Be grateful they're part of your team.

And it's always nice to show your appreciation for all their hard work. It doesn't have to be expensive. Send a box of cookies as a snack for the class. It's the thought that counts.

Get Involved At School

> *Some of us have great runways already built for us. If you have one, take off. But if you don't have one, realize it is your responsibility to grab a shovel and build one for yourself and for those who will follow after you.*
> *– Aviator Amelia Earhart*

If you possibly can, get involved with some of the school's activities. You don't have to join the Parent Teacher Association (PTA) full time, but it might be nice if you attended a meeting two or three times a year.

Some schools try to accommodate busy parents' schedules by having meetings and/or events during the day and evenings.

Network with other parents at school events and learn what they're working on with their children. Share tips and ideas, and be supportive of each other. You can make some new friends and may even find some potential "play dates" for your child. It's a win/win for everyone.

Know Your Rights

Your child is entitled to a good and appropriate education. If, for any reason, you are not satisfied with the educational plan and/or goals set for your child or you feel that your child's needs are not being met, you can seek to change the situation.

For example, there may be times when you feel that your child's teacher or therapists may not be the best "fit" for your child. Or there may be students in your child's class who may be harmful to or a bad influence for your child.

In situations like these, you should feel comfortable speaking to the school principal or other administrative personnel to resolve these issues.

Be Your Child's Best Cheerleader!

Make sure you celebrate your child's achievements, no matter how small. For example, if your child went from maintaining direct eye contact with you for one minute to three minutes, that's

> *Mankind owes to children the best it has to give.*
> *– Opening words of the UN Declaration of the Rights of the Child*

something to be happy about. Praise your child constantly and tell him/her that you're proud.

Every child has the potential to be "somebody" and their parents' support is essential for their growth.

And remember, academic ability is only part of a well-rounded child. Personal development – the growth of someone's personality and their unique characteristics – is also vital.

Don't limit your child to select activities that only an autistic or special needs child would or should do. Encourage him/her to explore the world around us, at home, school or in the community. It's a great way for your child to learn and grow.

YOU AND YOUR ADVISORY COUNCIL – Tapping Your Power Resources

Most parents in our situation find the overwhelming demands and constant pressures of autism cause them to doubt if they are always making the right decisions for their child. There can be that nagging thought in the back of your mind – "Am I really doing the smart thing here?"

> *When your mother asks, "Do you want a piece of advice?" it's a mere formality. It doesn't matter if you answer yes or no. You're going to get it anyway.*
> – Humorist Erma Bombeck

So, how can you be proactive and come up with good and appropriate solutions and strategies, when you have a million and one things on your mind?

Yes, it is possible, but you're going to need help. Your life is probably crazy enough as it is - you're too busy putting out fires to find innovative solutions to all your problems, never mind actually trying them out.

Well, we can't all have a village to help raise our child, but what you can have is an awesome **Autism Advisory Council**.

The purpose of the Council is to be a sounding board and resource for you. By having a group of dedicated, loyal and smart people who you can depend on, you won't feel so confused and stressed out with the immense responsibilities of caring for your child.

It's not as complex as it sounds, and the Council will help you take your battle plan to the next level as you enlist a powerful group of allies in your fight.

AUTISM ATTACK PLAN #8

Autism's Objective:

- **Prevent you from making the best, well-informed decisions for your child**

Autism's Tactics:

- **Overwhelm you with the huge and various responsibilities of raising your child**
- **Distract you so you'll be too busy to focus clearly on what's best for your child**
- **Make you doubt your abilities as a parent to make the smartest choices**

YOUR DEFENSE STRATEGY:

Capitalize On Your Resources

You may wonder where you are going to find these Council members and how you will find the time to form this group. You have a thousand things to do already and don't need another big job.

Well, the good news is that many of your Council members are in your life right now. These are the people you already turn to when you need solid advice or some help deciding programs or treatment for your child.

You'll find your Council members on the speed dial buttons of your cell phone and in your personal list of e-mail contacts. All you need to do is consolidate their contact information and file them as "autism council" in your computer. And take comfort in the fact that they are only a phone call or e-mail away.

Choose With Your Heart

An Advisory Council is only going to be as good as its members. That doesn't mean everyone has to be a genius or an expert, or a dear friend and ally. You need a mix of talents, types of relationships and areas of knowledge.

> *Sometimes, advice is what we ask for when we already know the answer, but wish we didn't.*
> – Writer Erica Jong

You will definitely want to have people you like or love and respect, such as friends and family members. In particular, make sure you have a good friend, family member or trained coach on board to provide the emotional support you may need when the "grief stages" and "nuclear side effects" start beating you down.

One important role of your Council is to help pick you up, restore your confidence and reassure you about the future.

Choose With Your Head

People who know and understand you personally will be a great help in deciding what strategies or solutions will work for you and your family.

However, you will need experts in medical professions such as pediatricians and neurologists to help you learn about, understand and select your treatment options.

Most parents only see their doctors when their child is sick. You can be proactive and have a medical professional on your Council to assist you in developing a good medical program for your child.

> *Go wisely and slowly. Those who rush oft stumble and fall.*
> – Playwright & poet William Shakespeare

And physicians are a great resource for many other things. They are constantly meeting with other medical professionals, attending medical conventions, reading journals and staying abreast of the latest medical procedures and treatments. Your doctor can consult with you on new treatments for autistic children and on health issues such as an innovative diet.

As well, look for experts in teaching and in various forms of therapy. They also attend conferences and seminars to update their skills and knowledge, so they can provide you with insight on new therapies and teaching methods that can benefit your child.

And, if you can get a favorite teacher or therapist on board – one that you have a good relationship with and who knows your child well – you will have a great ally and resource for your Council.

Take the Lead

The most important member of your Autism Advisory Council is you.

You need to be the leader. You're the one who sets the goals and uses all the advice from Council members to make your final decision.

> *Never lie in bed at night asking yourself questions you can't answer.*
> – Cartoonist Charles Schulz

The more informed you are, the better you can play that role and the more confidence you have that you are doing the best for your child. So, keep up-to-date on the latest research, services and programs.

There are many national and local organizations whose mission is to promote autism awareness and provide resources and information to families with special needs children. You can find them easily online and call for follow-up information.

Attend parent seminars, workshops and conferences. These are great places to network with autism experts, community educators and leaders as well as other parents.

In addition, some of these forums offer resource fairs where you can meet representatives from local government agencies who can provide information about benefits your child may be entitled to such as Social Security. There may also be companies and organizations that provide products and services for special needs children and their families.

Many of these conferences may be given by your child's school or local agencies that service the autism community in your city or state.

YOU AND YOUR BATTLE PLAN – Be the General!

That's a lot of information, isn't it? A battle plan for you, your family and your child is bound to be rather extensive.

Don't worry about trying to take it all in at once. Focus on the part that seems the most powerful or relevant to you and take it one step at a time.

And understand that your battle plan is bound to change as you grow in strength and confidence, and as your child's needs change over time.

The point is – you're on your way!

You are going from a potential casualty in the autism war to the general of your own small army, ready to fight and win!

Make no mistake, this really is a war and there will be battles won and lost. Autism will try to throw you off track and attack where you are weakest.

But, while you may take a bruise or a scratch here and there, autism will <u>never</u> be able to wound you again.

Now that you have the understanding of what has happened to you and your family, and how autism can affect you in the future, <u>you</u> can re-take control. <u>You</u> have the power!

You can reclaim your life …

You can fulfill your dreams …

You can be the best parent, spouse, friend and worker you can be …

You and your child can reach your potential …

And you and your family can have a good life – as good as anybody else's.

Now Go Out There and Fight!

▶AUTISM ARMY◀
ENLISTMENT FORM

I _____ hereby accept enlistment in the Autism Army,
(YOUR FULL NAME)

with the rank of General of Team _____.
(CHILD'S FIRST NAME)

In accepting this role, I pledge the following:

- ❖ **I will not allow autism to define or defeat me,**

- ❖ **I will see my child as a person, not a disability,**

- ❖ **I will strive for the best life possible for myself, as well as my child and my family,**

- ❖ **I will be the best champion, cheerleader, advocate and fighter for my child,**

- ❖ **I will not blame my child, myself or any other person for autism,**

- ❖ **I will treat myself, and the people around me, with the respect and patience we all deserve,**

- ❖ **I will not allow myself to become a casualty in the war against autism, and**

- ❖ **I will reclaim my life, re-take control and remain true to myself.**

You are now a soldier in the Autism Army. If you fail, you will try again until you succeed. If you fall, you will rise again, every time. You may weaken at times, but your strength will ALWAYS return.

You will stand tall and walk proud. You will lead your Team to victory. You will build a better future.

Congratulations, General!

SIGNATURE: DATE:

CONCLUSION

DID I TELL YOU HOW AMAZING YOU ARE?

TAKE A BOW – You Deserve It!

Well, it's been quite a journey, hasn't it?

We've gone from the shock and overwhelming impact of the diagnosis through the nuclear side effects autism has on you and your life, all the way to your battle plan for fighting back and reclaiming your life.

Now, I want to tell you something – if you're still standing after all that, you deserve a medal!

> *No matter where you are right now, no matter far along you are on your own path, don't wait to "have it all" to celebrate. You're never going to figure it all out. Make being happy your business, all along the way.*
> – Health food expert Bethenny Frankel

I know, because the war against autism knocked me off my feet and nearly did me in. It's taken 18 years of hard work to get where my family and I are today.

So, just taking on the challenge of raising a special needs child makes you a hero in my book. Nobody may ever carve a statue of you or name a street after you, but being a great parent always has to be its own reward.

And, yes, I just said you were a "great parent". How do I know?

Day in and day out, you are taking care of your autistic child. Thanks to you, they are getting to their doctors' and therapists' appointments. You're the one working with teachers and school staff to help ensure your child is getting an appropriate education. Because of you, your child's daily and personal needs are being met with care and love.

You're a rock star in your child's life and he or she would be lost without you. You deserve a national tribute for the heroic things you do on an everyday basis. Nobody's perfect, but you're pretty awesome!

KEEP YOUR PERSPECTIVE – This is YOUR Life

There's no getting around it, your child's autism has changed your life.

But nobody gets the life they expected. Lightning strikes, plans don't work out, things change. Everybody, with or without autism in their lives, ends up in a place they didn't expect, doing things they never thought they would.

The trick is to do the best with the life you have. With the right perspective and a good team, you will have a good life, and so will your whole family.

Yes, you have a child with autism. You may also have a child with red hair or a good singing voice or one thumb longer than the other. It is what it is – another unexpected turn on the unpredictable road of life.

We can't always control what happens to us, but we **can** change how we react. We can decide if autism is going to rule our existence, or if we are going to **take control, fight back and reclaim our lives**.

It's quite often just a matter of perspective.

A few years ago, offbeat director Tim Burton made a film version of Alice in Wonderland. In that movie, the Mad Hatter asks Alice if she thinks he really is crazy.

> In three words I can sum up everything I have learned about life; it goes on.
> – Poet Robert Frost

"Oh, yes," replies Alice, "You're <u>quite</u> insane! But don't worry, all the <u>best</u> people are!"

So, is your family "different" or outside the norm? Sure, absolutely. I know that my family looks like a mixed-up jumble of wild activity to outsiders.

But when people give me that look that says my family is odd, I think to myself, "I know, but all the <u>best</u> families are!"

Yours can be one of those "best" families, too. Take what you've got, enjoy what you can, fight where you must and make this the most wonderful life it can be!

ONE LAST STOP

The wild ride through stormy weather is over, the "Fix-It" tour is canceled, and your flight on Autism Airways is finally coming home.

There's just one last stop to make – a side trip to an amusement park.

There's a lot going on, but you and your Team have a plan ready to make sure everyone has the best time possible. It's a day of laughter with family and friends, including your child's teacher, therapist and pediatrician.

Now, when they go on the bumper cars, your family members work together and not against each other. When you ride the roller coaster, it's just for fun, not because your emotions are going up and down.

Everyone is doing their part to support each other while they enjoy the day. Your child is in the best hands possible and doing what all kids should do at an amusement park – having a blast!

You're sitting by yourself on a wooden bench near the merry-go-round, eating an ice cream and watching the summer sun begin to set over the nearby lake.

Suddenly, it dawns on you; all these people are here for your child.

And you silently think ... I am not alone anymore ... not afraid anymore ... not feeling weak or overwhelmed anymore. A big smile crosses your face.

The sun will set, the day will end and your ice cream won't last forever. But the memory of this moment will stay fresh ... part of the better life you are proud to have built.

And, tomorrow morning, the sun will come up again. Another day of challenges, but also another day of possibilities. You're going to make it the best day possible.

You finish off your ice cream, wipe off your hands and rejoin your family with a smile.

Author's Note:

Reclaiming your life is an ongoing process; you don't just do it once and stop working on it.

So, if you've found this book useful, keep it handy. Refer back to it when times get tough or when you feel yourself slipping backwards.

And my book should be just the beginning of your journey. Try every tool and resource that seems to make sense, then keep the ones that work for you and ditch the ones that don't.

You'll find a massive amount of information and advice on the Internet, including websites and free newsletters like mine (see www.YourAutismCoach.com). Just remember to take everything with a grain of salt - if it sounds too good to be true, it probably is.

And, if you decide to seek extra help from an autism coach like me, be sure to check out his or her credentials thoroughly, look at their client comments and references, and get to know him or her before making a decision. Legitimate coaches will offer a free introductory session to make sure they are the right fit for you and your family.

I sincerely hope that I've been able to help you through this book. If it makes the path a bit easier for parents of special needs children, I will be very proud and satisfied.

Deanna Picon

8175274R00055

Printed in Great Britain
by Amazon.co.uk, Ltd.,
Marston Gate.